Incredible Dating Adventures ...

NEXT!!

Live, Love, Laugh ...
And Sometimes Cry

Angela LaTorre

Incredible Dating Adventures ...
NEXT!!
Live, Love, Laugh ...
And Sometimes Cry

Angela LaTorre

www.IncredibleDatingAdventures.com

Copyright © 2010
Angela LaTorre Nickell

All Rights Reserved, including the right of reproduction, copying, or storage in any form or means, including electronic, In Whole or Part, without prior written permission of the publisher and author

Published by
CHB Media
3039 Needle Palm Drive
Edgewater FL 32141
(386) 690-9295
CHBmedia@gmail.com

ISBN-13: 978-0-9822819-2-5

First Edition
Printed in the U.S.A.

Contents

Welcome to Angie's World.......... v

Incredible Dating Adventures ... 1

Where Are You........................ 169

WELCOME TO ANGIE'S WORLD

Best wishes and happy reading. I'm delighted that you are joining me for what I hope you'll agree are some truly laughable dating adventures. While some of the events in this book may not have been funny at the time, they are all good for a laugh when looking back. Whether you read **NEXT!!** over a few hours or a few days, I think you'll agree that it's a joy ride through the always unpredictable landscape of women meeting and dating men for the first time. Whether the encounters I describe lasted for one date—or less—or went on a few weeks or months, these are stories of romance gone wrong. If you're looking for stories that end with bridal showers and white picket fences, you're in the wrong place! We're here to laugh out loud, smile and say, "Mama mia, can you believe these guys are real?" Well, let me assure you they are! Every last specimen of manhood on these pages is real! When you're done reading, you may ask, "Angie, where did you find these guys?" The unfortunate answer is that it wasn't difficult. I suppose I could have been more selective because I know there really are some good guys out there, but I was riding a learning curve that often felt like a bucking bronco.

With that fact in mind, this book is dedicated to every woman who has ever been involved in the challenges of dating. Whether you are in your twenties or well into your seventies, this book is for you. I have a strong feeling you may see yourself in some of my misadventures.

My name is Angela LaTorre Nickell and here's my story: I am a 54-year-old divorced business woman. I have been divorced for more than four years after a thirty-year marriage. I was married at a very young age and married the only man I ever dated. Yes, that's right—the only man, which made me a complete novice as far as the dating scene. Some of the men I met really took me to school! But don't feel sorry for me, I'm a fast learner. I took a few lessons, but I gave a few too!

PERSONAL PHILOSOPHIES

Post divorce syndrome was a very real (and traumatic) thing for me, and life after the divorce was a tremendous adjustment. During the most difficult times I often reflected on some of my personal philosophies so I could move on with my life. Hence the name of this book, "NEXT!!" As you will see as you read on, I was asking myself *what* is next for me, but also *who* is next for me. I thought I'd get an answer to the second question right away. It was not to be. I would say—or scream—NEXT! many times over those first years following my divorce.

Many of the personal philosophies regarding dating that I've learned over the past four years have proven themselves to be true time and time again. To begin with, *I believe that it's crucial that we represent ourselves as we really are.* This is always important, but so very important for good communication with the opposite sex. In the long run—and sometimes it doesn't take very long—all the truths will surface. It ends up being such a waste of time if honesty is not a focus.

In the quest to write my story I have read a few books along the way regarding "dating." I must admit my favorite is entitled *All the Rules*. I enjoyed the great wisdom the writer offered and learned the hard way the benefits of applying those rules, one of which is, "*rules girls* don't waste their time."

A second rule, especially important at this point of midlife, is never try to reinvent anyone or believe they will change. If his smoking bothers you early on when you are both on your best behavior, it will only get worse when you learn some of the not so great things "mister wonderful" is hiding. You must accept what you see.

It's important early on to "Look, Listen and Learn." Having two ears and one tongue is to our advantage. Listening twice as much as you talk is a great way to really get to know someone quickly. Ninety days seems to be a key timeline and taking a small trip after that period will usually tell the story. It's amazing what you learn when you travel with someone.

On a bit of a personal note I must share three valuable convictions I took from life-changing experiences, which helped me better understand people. These three concepts have been valuable in every aspect of my life.

The first one: *Take all the time required to get to know someone before you prejudge and assume they are who you think they are.* We—meaning women looking for a great guy in our lives—often see what we want to see. It takes a long time to really know someone. There are ways to accelerate the process, which is why I suggested the path of taking a short trip with them. And don't forget, prejudging can work two ways. My personal life lesson regarding this involved my beautiful daughter-in-law, Andrea. My only son, who I love so deeply, announced his engagement after meeting my soon-to-be daughter-in-law just twelve weeks prior. Of course, since she is from another country, I automatically assumed she had an agenda and I prejudged her before I allowed myself to get to know her. During this journey of understanding, which has resulted in a wonderful relationship for us, I've been amazed at how we manage to communicate even though language is such a barrier. But then, I shouldn't be surprised. Just think how we love and communicate with our pets, none of whom speak English—well, not much anyway!

My second suggestion: *When you think you are at the lowest, saddest point in your life, look around and take whatever scrap of positive energy you have in reserve and share it with someone who is in a worse place.* My older sister was diagnosed with cancer at the lovely age of thirty-six and was given nine months to live in 1991. She is still going strong to this day and has been a tremendous inspiration in my life in so many ways. Her two-year battle with this dreadful disease encompassed several surgeries, chemotherapy and radiation that left her exhausted. On one of my daily visits to the hospital I was startled and very upset to see her lying on her hospital bed totally bald and in a masculine looking hospital gown. At this extremely low point I thought to myself, "This can't be happening to our wonderful family." But the next day I came back and walked the halls determined to show strength. I had been staying for several days at the "Hope Lodge" and had seen such sadness from parents with small children battling cancer. At that point I decided to canvas the halls of the hospital and try to share some good positive cheer with people less fortunate than myself. It truly can help you conquer some of the darkest times in your life. Someone is always in a worse predicament than us, and the last thing anyone needs is for us to lose faith over misfortunes! With that in mind, you can see why my dating mishaps seem more like a comedy than a tragedy.

Finally: *Walk a mile or more in the shoes of someone who has gone through a life changing event before you even pretend to understand it.* For example, marriage and divorce must be experienced, not learned from a book. It's almost impossible to relate fully to a situation you have not personally experienced.

PERSONAL TRAITS

I've had this experience so often that I'm convinced it's true: every person you allow into your life will, for the most part, fall into one of four mathematical categories that correlate with their personality and reveal who they really are.

First on the list—and I thank God for them—are the "plus" personalities. Their specialty is addition, they add to your life. They are always glad to see you and you feel good while spending time with them and even better afterwards. Their compliments are always well received and people love being around them.

Now for one you want to try to avoid—the masters of subtraction, the "minus" personality. This personality is very toxic, draining, and extremely negative. They never seem to have a good day. They very often are critical and have a way of ruining your day. They simply can't allow you to be happy. This person is not a good travel buddy because of their constant discontent. Here's a great example of the negative personality that I recently experienced: I decided to meet an old girlfriend that I hadn't seen in six months at the mall on a Saturday to shop for a new spring wardrobe. I had gained eight pounds and she had lost twenty pounds. She parades herself around in her size six and makes it very obvious that you no longer are a size ten and on and on—you know the one I mean, we've all endured her. The worst part is you can't pacify her by saying how great she looks; she just has to tell you how bad you look.

Moving right along, we come to "the great divider." Although they may have some excellent attributes, they seem to always cause division in the crowd. They're the bad apple in the group, always stirring the pot, and can never go with the flow. They have a way of causing dissent and controversy in friendships, business relationships and family matters.

Last is "the amazing multiplier." This individual is the life of the party. People gravitate to them constantly and everyone wants to be there if he or she is present. They are excellent leaders but sometimes are just too busy socially to take the time to concentrate on your personal relationship with them.

Without question, given an opportunity, the "plus" personality is the one to invest the most time in.

My reason for sharing these thoughts, which apply to life in general and might well be a book by themselves, is to cause an awareness of these four personality types when dating. I can assure you it will be helpful. Of course, had I known then what I know now I might have avoided some of these mind-numbing dates altogether. But then where would I be? You can't just make this stuff up. As the old saying goes, truth is stranger than fiction.

I've developed a few more guiding principles during my four-plus years of dating. This one I've dubbed "HHH," meaning a happy heart for the home life. A good way to score points with me is to enjoy a somewhat normal relationship with your parents and kids, and to display as little family dysfunction as possible. A chaotic family history can greatly affect who the person is today.

I've also observed there are two kinds of people out there in this crazy single life: those who want to build and those who want to land. The "landers" are those who either have "rescue" written all over them, or are so co-dependent and unhappy with who they are that they need the companionship of someone around them all the time. "Builders" try to take the best of themselves and all they have to offer, and combine it with someone else's attributes to create a life together, slowly getting to know the other person in a spirit of honesty and integrity. When two "builders" work together, they can create a strong foundation that will withstand the challenges life often brings.

I like to think of building a relationship being like enjoying a fine five-course meal. You agree to meet and begin the process of discovery in a slow gentle way, just as you would make a slow, pleasurable journey of the meal. From the taste-kindling wine, to the encouragement of the appetizer and the palette neutralizing sherbet, and on to the main act—the entrée, and then finally the dessert, each step is taken with patience, consideration, and appreciation for pleasure. If it's truly a fine meal, you'll discover it along the way.

JUST FOR FUN

I mentioned in the introduction having read about "Rules Girls" and how they operate when it comes to dating. Since I'm not all that good at keeping the rules, I call my rules "Just for Fun" rules. Since I occasionally broke my rules, I admit they are more like suggestions than commandments. My "Just for Fun" thoughts will pop up throughout the book. Here's a few of them. He cannot be:
- Shorter than me,
- Weigh less than me, or
- Be prettier than me.
- He can take his eyes out at night (contacts) but if the teeth come out, we are done.
- A Just for Fun Fact: My shortest date lasted a grand total of nineteen minutes.

DEDICATION

I dedicate this book to all the single women of America, especially those looking for romance the "second time around." Or third. Or fourth. Whether you are twenty-two or eighty-nine, live, love, laugh and try not to cry too often as you go through life's dating adventures. I raise a glass to all the single women of today who are greeted by Mr. Wonderful with a dead daisy from his backyard, and to all the women who have been afflicted with men so cheap they suggest you order from the children's menu on the first date and tell you it would be to your benefit since you need to lose ten pounds. Or how about the guys who brag about being gourmet cooks but then proceed to open the flip top on a Vienna Sausage can, or want to share a single reheated chicken breast along with a can of store brand green beans for dinner on a Friday night? Date long enough and you'll meet all these characters. I did, but because I approach life with love and laughter, I lived to tell about it!

A special dedication to my lovely daughter-in-law, Andrea. I only need one like her. She has made my son a very happy man and a father of two incredibly handsome boys. My prayer is that someday my grandsons will read this book and be more compassionate men because of it. Matthew Sebastian and Austin Frabizo, Nona will always love you.

■ ■ ■

So let's get started: Every man will be categorized by chapter; some chapters will discuss more than one. I will with respect keep all of them nameless and, at the end of each chapter, highlight their good points—if I can think of any—as this is meant to be positive, fun reading.

The final chapter, entitled "Where Are You?" will reveal how little I knew when I first journeyed forth to find the man of my dreams—the perfect man who I now know does not exist. **Bon Voyage!** I hope your trip is shorter than mine.

THE ADVENTURES ARE ...

The Handyman Special	Page 1
Internet Madness	Page 5
The Swinger	Page 17
Tall Dark and Then Some	Page 21
Dumber Than Dumb	Page 27
The Seasoned Gentleman	Page 33
Elvis Has Left the Building	Page 37
The One That Got Away	Page 41
The Biker	Page 45
The Scam Artist	Page 49
Facing Myself	Page 55
The Alcoholic	Page 61
The Jealous One	Page 67
Match.com and The Surfer	Page 75
The Charmer	Page 81
The Cheap Heart Throb	Page 87
The Herbologist	Page 93
The Holy One	Page 97
The Dancer	Page 99
Man and His Dogs	Page 103
Man and His Hair	Page 109
Momma's Boy	Page 115
Blind Date Horrors	Page 121
More Internet Madness	Page 129
Bar Scene Lies	Page 139
Easy Pick-ups & the Player	Page 147
Mr. Money Bucks	Page 153
The English Delight	Page 159
The Gator	Page 161
A Hopeful Finale	Page 167
Where Are You?	Page 169

Definition: hand•y•man spe•cial
(noun) 1) property needing repair. 2) property that is attractively priced because it needs extensive repairs beyond the ability of most people. 3) broken down.

THE HANDYMAN SPECIAL

Most of us, men and women, have something about which we are more proud than we deserve to be. I guess that's true of almost every man I will talk about in the coming chapters. Their mothers are probably to blame. Being so proud of their own accomplishment in child birth, they convey a sense of exceptionality to their little boys, who never really face the facts enough to become real men. Just a thought. I generally left their delusions in tact for the next women to deal with (sorry girls). Self delusion was surely a trait of the "Handyman Special." Here's his story, the first bump on my rocky road.

My divorce was final in May and I was forty-nine rapidly approaching the big "five-zero." Fifty is a turning point in any woman's life: time to assess, redefine and evaluate. We all know the stereotypes about men at fifty: they get a new

NEXT!!

head of hair-implants if they have money and a cheap rug if they don't, often one so tacky that you wonder if they have mirrors in their house. Or it's a sports car; again it's something nice like a *Corvette* or *Mercedes* if they have money or an old beat up sixties-era *Mustang* if they don't. Of course they'll claim they bought the old *Mustang* because they "just love spending hours restoring cars," while in fact they ought to be spending hours in the gym restoring themselves! Don't get me wrong, I wasn't necessarily searching for someone rich or perfect, just an honest guy with a little concern for his appearance.

Back to my point: women reassess at fifty just like men, and there's nothing like divorce to get the process started. So, in the midst of rebounding from my divorce and facing fifty, I decided to take up my life-long passion for ballroom dancing. Feeling lonely and somewhat vulnerable, I put aside my fears, got myself dressed up and looking desirable (I don't mind saying) and headed off to attend my first "Singles Dance" as a single woman. As I enter the door I am instantly engulfed with attention from ..."The Handyman." I'm not complaining mind you, it was better than standing there alone with no one to talk to, feeling like the wallflower girl at a middle school sock hop. I guess I had just imagined someone different, OK, better, much better!

But back to brutal reality. Here comes Mr. Handyman: In his mid-sixties, on the short side but rather good looking. What could I lose by dancing with him, except maybe, as it turned out, a few of my toes? As he awkwardly led me around the floor, he regaled me with tales of his expertise with a hammer and a saw, along with some other tools I figured only a true handyman would know about. Who would have thought a man could imagine carpentry to be such a romantic subject? His dancing was nothing to write

Angela LaTorre

home about, but I was sure his wood-working prowess would make me gasp in appreciation. Think again sisters.

For a handyman one would expect—I did anyway—that his one-room A-frame home would at least have drywall! You may be thinking, "Oh, you saw the inside of this pathetic man's house did you?" Yes, I accepted his invitation to dinner the very next night. I knew he wasn't perfect, but ... well, I was ... lonely.

I had never before experienced eating dinner with rolled insulation stacked around me everywhere I looked. Between worrying the fibers from the pink stuff would get in my food, the sight of exposed beams and no air conditioning, I quickly lost my appetite. Fortunately, I got an opportunity to leave the table when his neighbors came pounding on his door. The irate couple was shouting from outside, "We are sick and tired of you parking your damned old truck in front of our house with the wheels on our lawn!"

> ... there is nothing pretty about seeing a man strike an old woman ...

"They're always hasslin' me about something," he said. "I'm just tryin' to give my grass a chance to grow."

What grass, I wondered; his front lawn was as bare as his walls. When he didn't jump up to move his truck, the neighbors returned. That first and only date with him ended then and there. As I climbed into my car, from the corner of my eye I could see the Handyman was pretty handy with his fists. He had knocked the older man to the ground and was turning on the woman, who had been beating him in the back of the head with a wooden spoon. I don't know, maybe she was making dinner when her husband dragged her out to help confront their neighbor. I turned away—there's nothing pretty about seeing a man strike an old woman—all

NEXT!!

the while thinking that as soon as I get out of here I better grab my cell phone and call 9-1-1. As I backed out of the driveway, I saw he had only grabbed the spoon from her. Thank God, I thought, and drove away just as fast as I could go, thinking, for the very first time on this adventure— **NEXT!!**

  Good points: None, accept that he never called me again. Come to think of it, I'm not sure he even had a phone.

Angie's Lessons Learned ...

Not everyone has traveled the same distance on the evolutionary scale.

"For you to ask advice on the rules of love is no better than to ask advice on the rules of madness."
~ Terence, Roman poet and philosopher

INTERNET MADNESS

Oh the internet! How it has changed our world and made our world a smaller place. Being able to talk to some young "studly" guy claiming to live in Africa via the internet is amazing but not for me, what's the point? How often have those dreamy first date scenarios existed only on the computer screen with zero courage exhibited as far as agreeing to meet you for a glass of wine.

It seems like the internet really has turned the rules of love into the rules of madness, and the first victim has been the truth. I am amazed by the guys that all seem to be posing in front of the same red "jag." Is there a *Jaguar* owning photographer out there traveling around doing these shots? If not, it's a good business idea. Roll into town, shoot five or six supposed bachelors in front of the car, and then off to the next venue. The next month make the same circuit in a *Bentley*.

NEXT!!

Or what about the guy who is standing in front of high-end furniture from Rob and Stuckey from which someone has forgotten to remove the tags? One of my best friends had a brilliant idea. She was so tired of all the internet lies about age, she now requests that her prospect post a photo holding the daily newspaper with the date clearly visible. Another friend said she dropped all the high-priced dating services and started shopping on Craig's List. Instead of one date a week she's now averaging at least one a day. In fact she had so much trouble fitting them all in she once had three dates in one day. If I was going to give her experience its own chapter, I might call it "Breakfast, Lunch and Dinner," although from what she said, the better name would be "Three Strikes and You're Out." At least *Craig's List* is free. Another option for free searching is *www.PlentyofFish.com*; trust me there truly are many fish in the sea. Someone might say you get what you pay for, but as I was about to learn, quality is hard to find no matter where you shop … or "fish" as the case may be.

Hopefully, this statement won't earn a call from lawyers for that pricey dating service you see on TV, but it seems wherever you shop you can find chuck steak posing as filet mignon. I have nothing against chuck steak—it can be tasty, but it should be labeled as what it is.

I must be fair and say that at first my negative impressions of internet dating came entirely from friends, not experience. But every once in a while I'd hear someone say they met their new spouse online, "and we couldn't be happier." They would recommend this site or that as being reputable. All and all, I was admittedly curious and decided to venture out into the strange world of cyberspace dating.

Turning fifty was close at hand along with Labor Day Weekend and I desperately wanted a date. You know the feeling. It often arises around New Year's Eve or when a close friend is getting married and your ex-husband will be there with his new wife. *Match.com* was calling and calling, offering their complimentary initial trial month. A simple photo and short profile of me generated several responses including "Good Guy 99". First red flag: he has been on *Match.com* since 1999 and it's now 2005. Additional flags: negative statements regarding his two ex-wives, and the last good book he read was the manual to his hot rod *Mustang*. But his age was right and, in his own opinion, "Joe" was an excellent dancer. When the night was over, I looked in the mirror and said, "You must have really needed a date."

"Good Guy 99" arrives on time and so does the overkill of Old Spice. I am instantly reminded of my deceased grandfather. Surprise, surprise, and double surprise, the photo was old and the hair was gone along with his back end. What hair was left was aiming North with the help of a serious gob of some gummy gel. The flowers, however, were beautiful.

We were soon off to a local casual restaurant. No problem, except that his map quest directions were not accurate. I tried to help but received firm resistance. What do I know, I've only lived in this town since 1973. We finally arrived and were greeted by a rather sun-damaged waitress who acted like she had wanted to go home an hour earlier and was beyond pretending she was happy to wait on us. (It may sound tacky to mention her skin issues but it often seemed to me that when these bad dates started sliding downhill, every little detail would fit right in, as if someone had written a script ... and as a medical aesthetician I notice skin concerns first.) She asked for our order and he instantly responded for me, saying, "No, we are not interested in having a glass of wine." He ordered his ice water; I was en-

NEXT!!

joying my ice tea when, much to my amazement, I was told that since "we both are not that hungry" I shouldn't mind sharing a meal with him. Where he got that idea, I don't know. I'm stunned, but I agree, having been raised to always demonstrate impeccable manners.

On my suggestion, a four-shrimp appetizer was reluctantly approved and before the plate hit the table he helped himself to three of them. At this point he is beginning to display affection and says he can feel that we are connecting "in a special way." I'm wondering what in the world I'm doing here. After enjoying one shrimp, four French fries and a fish filet—enough to feed a cat—I am once again instructed that we will not be having dessert. When the check arrived "Good Guy 99" looked at the bill and says, "Angie, I didn't bring my glasses so can you add in the tip and tell me what my half is?" At that point, I should have made a fast dash for the door but, but ... I thought, what if he really is a great dancer? I was such a fool in those days, and, I can admit now, so frightened of being alone and unwanted.

> ... I was getting a case of internet fever. If you've had it, you know what I mean ...

Well, so much for dinner. The hot rod Mustang was longing to hit the road and take us to a singles ballroom dance. It's August of 2005 and the country is recovering from Hurricane Katrina with sky high gas prices. His conversation is now focused on the fee for the dance. I guess his half of the restaurant bill, totaling $11.52, was still affecting him. I casually mentioned it would be either seven or ten dollars each depending on whether a DJ was playing or a band. We arrive and I'm dropped at the front door during a dreadful thunderstorm and proceed to pay for both of us. He comes in behind me as I am signing a credit card slip for twenty-three dollars that includes two bottles of water. God knows I needed Vodka instead! He hands me seven dollars. Oh well, maybe he is a great dancer! That turns out to be another bad joke. Two left feet is an understatement. I spotted some great friends from past visits and we agreed to dance with other people, thank God. Finally, it's closing time and I'm thankful the DJ has a sense of humor. He plays "Hit the Road Jack" as the final song. Laughter was exactly what I needed. Glad the night is almost over, I grab my "Good Guy 99" and am now audibly singing the words to him. But he is not connecting with my message.

The ride home was long but the hot rod Mustang was up to it. Fortunately, it was also loud so I didn't have to force any conversation. I offer gas money while he offers Tic Tacs. No thank you, I am newly divorced, I tell him, and not interested in kissing anyone at this time. Of course I would have kissed him if I'd wanted to but his chances ended with the ice water and shrimp grab. He dropped me in my driveway in the pouring rain. I am instantly soaked as I watch him peel out, not even waiting to make sure I got inside. What a night! Two days later I received an e-mail stating, "had a great time can't wait for our next date." **NEXT!!**

Good points: Pretty flowers; they lasted a week.

So I had one bad experience but internet dating was still intriguing me. In fact, I was getting a case of internet fever. If you've had it you know what I mean. The messages and flirts from men were starting to stack up in my inbox and suddenly I'm feeling like the most popular girl at the ball! "Well I do declare Rhett darling, my dance card seems to be full!" I couldn't stop now. So I get really brave and start sending out flirts of my own.

A guy I've nicknamed "The Studly One" responded and the e-mailing back and forth went well. He was relocating to

NEXT!!

Central Florida from Texas where he is employed as a tennis pro, or so he leads me to believe. Forty-nine years old, he claims. He's coming to check out a job and a place to live and will be staying with a friend. We agree to meet. I'm excited and optimistic, but I find him frantically pacing in the parking lot as he waits for me. My excuse, which I couldn't tell him, was it took me a while to pick him out because he was a little hard to spot. On a good day with heels he was maybe five-foot-six, three inches shorter than stated in his profile. Five minutes into the conversation over ice water we somehow lost ten years. Actually, I should say we gained ten years, but isn't a gain usually something good? He was really fifty-nine but felt that he didn't look it so why not lie. The house salad was tasty and the conversation uncovered the following facts: He's not a tennis pro, he plays with some local pros; he does not have a job but hopes to find one in Florida after he sells his furniture from *Big Lots*, says goodbye to his roommate in Texas and sells his 1992 *Buick*. The keys in his hand, he finally admits, belong to his friend's car that he borrowed for an hour to meet me. A rental car for his two-week stay in Florida was not included with the free rent.

Good luck and goodbye. Look, I was seeking a stable kind of guy, but my list of attributes in a man does not require he be famous, wealthy or a tennis pro. It does include being honest. If a man views me as a woman so shallow that she needs to be deceived, what does that signify for the future? Two weeks later I received an e-mail from him casually stating, "You're not going to find anyone as well rounded as me with so much to offer in little Central Florida. Oh, and guess what Angie, I came home to two unwelcome 'welcome-back' surprises. A letter from the IRS for delinquent taxes in the amount of $322, and a bill for $150 to have the window

fixed on my 1992 *Buick*." **NEXT!!**
Good point: he did pay the <u>entire</u> $14.52 lunch bill.

Well, they say the third one is the charm. I'm feeling more than a little frustrated with the internet guys but this one is not an internet blind date; he is an acquaintance of a friend of mine. But she's obviously a friend who does not know me very well. First impressions happen within twenty seconds but this broke the record. Ten seconds was all I needed. "Mr. Wonderful" is rocking on the porch at our local *Cracker Barrel*, with the Blue Tooth in his ear glowing and ringing at the same time. Apparently he's a man of great importance as the ear glowed during the entire lunch. What was not glowing however was his personality. His arrogant, better than you attitude toward the waitress was a huge turn off. My final exit became inevitable when I saw him use the side of his hand to scoop his mash potatoes onto his fork. **NEXT!!**
Good point: I love the apple pie ala mode and diet root beer at *Cracker Barrel*.

I'm jumping forward now to the fall of 2007 when I decided to give the internet one more try. What could it hurt? Hunting for the right man had begun to feel like an adventure and people were starting to say, "You ought to write a book." Since my last internet escapade I'd dated numerous men I had met in person one way or another, and frankly, I couldn't see that the guys met online were any worse. But I suppose it was the fact that I had acquired some great pictures of myself that convinced me to try the internet dating sites again.

I am sometimes easily lured by opportunities that sound amazingly wonderful. A small modeling agency in my charming beach town convinced me that there is a huge demand

NEXT!!

for models that are middle-aged and not a size six. With my great hair, nice smile and somewhat curvy hips, they convinced me to do a photo shoot, assuring me I would be loved by agents looking for size ten to twelve models because "as you know we are the buying population." The session was fun, and they definitely have a way of making you look fabulous on photo paper. Three months later, my time, postage and letter writing to over thirty agents had resulted in zero responses as far as potential modeling goes. The good news was at least I didn't get any rejection letters—just no responses at all. I have a really hard time with rejection, so that was good, and the search for modeling jobs kept my mind off the search for men.

Well, after about another month and contemplating *Match.com* once again, I decided why not? Nothing's happening here as far as potential prospects, and the local pubs are not my thing. I had these wonderful photos but no man, so in early August I put myself out there once again. In one week I had three hundred men view my profile and had about 175 e-mails. It's amazing how everyone sounds so wonderful and looks awesome online. After reviewing all the e-mails and discounting the 35-year-olds, the ones clear across the country or in another country, the ones flexing their biceps, sporting tattoos or baseball caps worn backwards, standing in elegantly furnished rooms or with expensive cars where the picture was mostly of the room or the car, and finally the guy who said his favorite hobby is going the flea market, I ended up with four prospects. After much telephone conversation (carefully using a telephone card so they didn't have my number), followed by confirmation of their info on *USA people search.com*, I agreed to meet each of them—one at a time of course— at a local night spot. Numbers one and two were still too bitter and consumed

Angela LaTorre

with their ex-wives, their kids and money issues. No thanks! Number three presented himself thirty minutes late, ten years older than his photo, and about thirty pounds heavier. As he approached, he loosened his sweaty shorts as his large frame shifted from left to right. He announced his arrival by saying, "I told you to meet me at the bar." He was holding the largest glass of beer I'd ever seen in one hand while I shook the other. I quickly ate my appetizer and paid the bill myself, after he stated he was not hungry and only planned on beer, and left the restaurant post haste. I won't even tell you about number four. I'm still trying to forget.

Two months later, after some good conversation I agreed to meet another prospect: forty-seven, never married and very involved in technology, leisurely in his way of speaking, and working as a professional "Software Architect." He had intelligence of a kind I later came to call "software brains." Our date was programmed into his GPS. The problem was he entered "street" in the address instead of "drive." No big deal as this charming little New Smyrna Beach can be conquered in a matter of hours on a bicycle and once you arrive on the barrier island we call "beachside," you know for sure when you have left. As the classic saying goes, all roads lead to Rome.

Ten minutes before our agreed meeting time, he called with obvious frustration in his voice and a few choice words about my town. His technology had failed him and he was lost, but was not about to admit any fault. I graciously offered to help direct his way. We were only three minutes and two miles from each other but time goes by and my "techie" is nowhere to be seen. I went outside to visually survey the situation and as I approached the parking lot my phone rang. He states, "I circled the parking lot three times and did not find a place to park so I am on my way back

NEXT!!

home (an hour away) and maybe we will make it another time." He then hangs up without giving me a chance to speak. Since I was standing in an empty parking spot and looking at numerous others, I decided to return his rather abrupt call and assure him of a place to park, and if he chose not to turn around, there most definitely would not be "another time." I was beyond words when he said, "that's fine." My response: "No problem!" **NEXT!!**

In my professional work, I have a collection of amazing clients, many of whom are single women with the same quest for finding a quality man. On occasion as I am rejuvenating their skin we share some of our stories. Well, Miss Geneva thought she had met a nice "seasoned" gentleman in his mid-seventies. They enjoyed their first meet and greet at Denny's on Senior Night. Along with the free dessert because it was his birthday, he, of course, also had a coupon. No problem, there's nothing wrong with being frugal. The waitress offered to put the remains of Miss Geneva's cheeseburger in a doggy bag but she said no thank you. The birthday boy had enjoyed his burger down to the last bite and was busy lining up his coupons to quietly pay the bill when the waitress came back to finish clearing the table. "I think I'll take home the rest of her cheeseburger," he said. Well of course, she was amazed. When she finished her story there was a moment of silence in the shop, then we looked at each other and with a good laugh said together, "NEXT!!"

Laughter rang through the shop and another client, a lovely professional woman who has been single for many years shared two amazing stories. She agreed to meet a potential "companion" introduced by a friend and on their first date he proceeded to tell her that she could definitely stand to lose ten pounds and asked the waitress to bring her the children's menu. "NEXT!!" Now we were all in tears as we shared our laughter and misery. "I have more," she said. On a separate occasion, the same friend decided to try again, this time fixing her up with a man she knew casually from the office. He invited my client to his house for his version of a casual diner and announced he will be preparing a gourmet meal using some of his famous recipes. He would say only that the entree will include beef. As he opens a can of Vienna Sausage links, she gently confessed that she wasn't feeling well all of a sudden and must leave. As she completed telling her tale, she didn't have to add, "never to return." We all understood. One of my great joys in compiling these stories is that I've learned how much I share with the sisterhood—both the horror stories and the determination to keep believing "Mr. Right" is out there waiting ... somewhere.

Angie's Lessons Learned ...
Catalogue shopping is risky. Shopping for a man without seeing the goods is suicide.

"If there's one pitch you keep swinging at and keep missing, stop swinging at it"
~ Anonymous
"It don't mean a thing if it ain't got that swing."
~ Duke Ellington

THE SWINGER

The ballroom dance community has a special mystique. It's a wonderful place for immersing yourself in a kind of extreme physical activity that's also very passionate. In fact, blood-pumping passion is what makes the experience of ballroom dancing special. But if that was the entire story, I wouldn't be writing about it. After all, this isn't a beginner's guide to dance. The ballroom isn't just about dancing, it's about romancing. And it attracts some very interesting characters, which leads me into another fun-filled chapter that spells "passion" with a capital **P** and "romance" with a capital **R**. At least it started out that way.

The third Saturday of every month a particular dance hall in the Orlando area hosts a singles dance that always draws about three hundred people. An hour into the dance, in walks "The Swinger." He's dressed in a complete three-piece

NEXT!!

suit, every hair is in place and his *Chiclets* smile is glowing. His approach is smooth, the cologne is rich, and his dancing is adequate. Before long he had turned an average night of dance into a special night of dance, and as we moved around the floor I learned he was a business man managing and running his own printing company. I must admit I was attracted. He seemed to have his act together and said almost everything I wanted to hear. I was already warming to him, imagining the possibilities, when he capped the night by expressing his strong spiritual values and convictions regarding life. What more could I ask? He was a true prospect and I wasn't going to let it end that night on that dance floor. This one was worthy of a date. We booked a return engagement.

Date night came, and reservations, candles and a nice downtown Daytona Beach restaurant had us both feeling comfortable. Actually, we were beyond comfortable. When I look back on that evening, I'm amazed at how I let myself get caught up in believing, but you have to remember what—and who—I'd been through since my divorce.

> It suddenly was apparent that all the calls regarding "church" were no more than a cover-up.

There I was sitting at a somewhat exotic restaurant on Daytona's Beach Street, a far cry from dining on canned sausages among stacks of pink insulation in a broken down shack. Outside is the romantic riverfront; inside all the couples around us are just like us—feeling the night's tender passions. The atmosphere carried me away. And here was a guy who was smooth and knew how to charm. So forgive my naiveté.

But between the appetizer and the main course his cell phone started ringing. I soon learned that several of his "lady friends" were calling regarding plans for church the next morning—and specific happenings afterwards. As I am watching and learning and feeling somewhat neglected, and beginning to feel the conversations were becoming a little bit too intimate, daylight began to shine on my romantic night fantasies. What I hear him discussing doesn't seem to be leading to an after-church "dinner on the grounds."

We finished our dessert and coffee and the good news is this one at least paid the bill. As we begin walking outside I'm feeling like I'm about to be written out of the script, but he reaches for my hand and starts to get real close. He begins kissing me on the cheek and then mentions there is something very important he needs to get out of his red 2000 stretch Lincoln. Something I might enjoy.

He dashes off and comes back to me wearing a smile the size of Kansas. He hands me a stack of photos and says, "take a look and enjoy, Angela."

Much to my amazement, before my innocent eyes are pictures of all his escapades involving women and men, and in most cases more than two at a time, shot from different angles, etc. etc.

Oh my God! It finally hits me: He is a SWINGER and all of it is being coded in the name of "God!" It was suddenly apparent that all the calls regarding "church" were no more than a cover-up. Not that he and his friends never spent any time on their knees.

Talk about taking the Lord's name in vain! Or would this fall under the commandment about keeping the Sabbath? **NEXT!!!**

Good points: The Mongolian cuisine was excellent, and he at least didn't waste any time coming to the point. After years working in a salon, you'd think I'd know about stuff like this and I suppose I'd heard stories. But this was my first

NEXT!!

time getting a first-hand education! At least this was one dating episode I had no trouble laughing about, and a guy I had no trouble forgetting about.

Angie's Lessons Learned ...

For some people, when it comes to sex, too much is never enough.

"The first time you buy a house you see how pretty the paint is and buy it. The second time you look to see if the basement has termites. It's the same with men."
~ Lupe Velez, Mexican Film Actress

TALL, DARK AND THEN SOME

Well, my next dating experienced involved a very tall, dark and handsome man. He was all of six-foot-eight and would turn heads everywhere we went. I don't want to sound small-minded about short men; they often work harder at relationships and that is so appreciated. But when you are a tall woman, there is something to be said for tall men, although I'll admit that sometimes, like beautiful women, tall men can take the physical gifts they've been given as a form of privilege and entitlement. That often leads to arrogance, another word for selfish pride, which the good book says "goes before the fall."

True to form, Mr. "Tall, Dark and Then Some" was pretty full of himself. He didn't think he had to play by the same rules as everyone else. Thought he could get away with just about anything. I'll have more on what that means in just a moment. He also had a whole list of medical problems, which troubled me at first, but they paled as a concern when I saw the issues he had with his temper. The temper really began to show as we reached the third or fourth week of dating.

Being from an Italian family, I'd seen men with tempers before. They flare and then die down. So it wasn't an absolute deal breaker for me, since he also was fun, musical, and had a nice family. And truthfully it wasn't him showing his temper that ended our relationship. His final exit came when he decided we all needed to see another one of his personal traits—namely his personal anatomy.

Before I get to that, since I've already risked disapproval by dishing out generalizations about short men, tall men, beautiful women, tall women and Italian men, let me add just one more: the sexual attitudes of divorced middle-aged women returning to the dating scene. Someone (hopefully) may have noticed that I dated "Tall, Dark and Then Some" for at least three or four weeks. It was actually longer than that. None of my other dates to that point lasted more than one night past our initial encounter. So you might be wondering, "Did they get intimate?" And, just what is the meaning of the phrase "then some?"

> I've heard many women say that after their divorce that they plan to take it slow with sex, but very few of them actually do.

If any of my sisters want to tell me I'm wrong about this, well, go to my web site and lodge a complaint, but I think some behaviors are hard to reverse. After 20 or 30 years in a marriage, maybe even giving birth, sexual activity (if it exists at all!) takes on certain forms and expectations. It's like playing tennis. When you first start to play, you might be happy to casually hit the ball around. But after a while you start to play some matches, take it seriously and play for keeps; you like to really go at it and work up a sweat. There's very little chance you're going to walk on the court and tell your partner, "Oh, let's just hit the ball around a little today." It's hard to go back. And, barring injury, you're not going to stop before the set is over.

I've heard many women who begin to date again after failed marriages say they plan to take it slow with the men they meet and institute a lengthy, mandatory waiting period. But few of them actually enforce the original plan. What was it the poet Robert Burns said about "the best laid plans of mice and men...?" Careful plans often give way to the twists and turns of real-world circumstances. Life is like that. So often we try to make life match exactly with our wishes, but there are just too many variables to be controlled. And sometimes a totally surprising stroke of good luck comes our way. Don't go jumping forward, but I think you'll agree that the way my story plays out proves that point. At least it proved it to me.

Back to the anatomy lesson: It was a hot, balmy August night in Titusville, which is near Cape Canaveral about forty miles south of my home. We were off to celebrate a friend's fortieth birthday. "Tall, Dark and Then Some" had quite a collection of friends and this particular guy had another best buddy with the same birthday. More than seventy guests were enjoying the evening in all its wonder, with a full bar being one of the highlights. We had been dating long enough for him to feel comfortable about me joining him as he had classified himself as "Angie's new boyfriend."

The guest list included some fairly prominent people: future political hopefuls, attorneys, business men and woman, physicians—even some of my very own clients. The party theme was "BEER" and it was flowing everywhere you

NEXT!!

looked, along with the full bar. The birthday bash was highlighted by an incredible full-busted cake that would have made Mae West proud. All in all it was a full-blown blast, and all done in good taste with everything you would want: warm weather, great music and food, alcohol of course, and thank God, lots of people with a great sense of humor. Everywhere you looked, laughter pierced the air.

After several hours of awesome food, music, and beer, the warm humidity of the evening set in for the tall one's two buddies—along with the thrill of making it to forty together, having shared memories since elementary school. They decided it was time to jump in the pool and on impulse to celebrate in their own special way by becoming "a bit too comfortable," if you know what I mean. I watched in amazement, delighted to see the pool was lit ever so slightly by a gleam of moonlight.

As the fun, laughter, and loud music continued, most of the crowd decided we all needed to toast the long time buds from Titusville, also known on occasion as "Tits-ville." With the cheers came thoughts of cooling off. Decorum was definitely out the window and in my somewhat menopausal state and in the midst of another raging hot flash the pool was calling. In an effort to include "the tall one" in the fun, I became insistent in my attempts to persuade him to jump in as well. But to my great surprise, his infamous temper took over and some choice words flew my way. At that point, "Mr. Tall, Dark and Then Some" decided to "drop his draws" as they say in Kentucky and expose his virtuous jewels. I was totally embarrassed in front of all those people. I looked up and caught the eye of a woman I had enjoyed getting to know a bit that evening and said to myself, "Another one bites the dust." I gave him a large piece of my mind and informed him this was our last date. **NEXT!!**

Good points: He actually had many, but that raging temper and surprising public exposure ruled them out of further consideration.

> **Angie's Lessons Learned ...**
> A man being prone to sudden rage should be No. 1 on a girl's list of dating red flags.

"I'm not offended by dumb blonde jokes because I know I'm not dumb. I also know I'm not blonde."
~ Dolly Parton, American singer and actress

DUMBER THAN DUMB

Growing up in a big fun-loving Italian family has a list of benefits longer than the pasta column on an Italian restaurant menu. One of the best of those benefits is a load of cousins. Well one of my favorites and I must say a great girl, is Cousin Kathy. She is beautiful, witty, very successful and her voice has been heard over many broadcast airways. Kathy decided I needed to meet this great gentleman with whom she has had the pleasure of doing a few real estate transactions. He was the right age, seemed to have somewhat of a job, had never been married and—based on her good judgment—was someone I thought I'd like to meet. An initial meet and greet was planned at her office. He showed up looking like he just got off the farm but still, I told myself, he seemed rather personable and would probably clean up well. I now think I gave him too much benefit of the doubt because of the Kathy connection.

NEXT!!

It's the weekend before Easter and my son and his in-laws are due in that weekend. Being the Italian mother that I am, I always make my son's favorite Italian lasagna when he comes to visit. I made the largest pan of lasagna my oven would hold, to be shared with some co-workers as well. When this new gentleman called and invited me to dinner the Friday before my son's visit I suggested that he enjoy a good home-cooked meal, a rare delight for a bachelor. He was thrilled and after a lengthy conversation we decided he would arrive at 6:30 for dinner, hopefully bringing a nice bottle of wine or whatever his preference for a beverage was. I made it very clear that smoking was a concern of mine and he promised, in so many words, that he was working seriously on a plan to quit. Of course, somehow it came out in the conversation that yellow flowers, especially roses, were my favorite. Simple directions to my town home concluded the conversation.

> He presents me with a limp yellow daisy pulled from his yard, roots and all ...

That afternoon, after preparing, I set a lovely table and divided up the oversized lasagna, taking some to share with co-workers. I left a designated portion of the tasty dish on the stove for that evening. My beloved, now deceased, beautiful black lab somehow managed to enjoy a good portion of the tasty lasagna while I was at work that afternoon. I carefully managed to salvage enough for my latest prospect's portion and hoped that black hairs would not be sticking out of the white ricotta cheese.

My date was to arrive at 6:30 p.m. and of course he did not have a cell phone or a computer—he simply "did not believe in either one." As 7:15 approached I began to wonder, worry and think, "Oh my God another interesting story is about to unfold." Exactly an hour and a half later, the door

Angela LaTorre

bell rings and there stands the evening's "Mr. Wonderful," later to be known as "Dumber than Dumb." No, it didn't occur to him to stop at a pay phone and call. He has driven by my home numerous times, stopped to enjoy the Atlantic Ocean but just never, not once, thought to call. Didn't realize it was a problem, he says. Also didn't occur to him that he has anything for which to apologize.

I know I'm not perfect, but enough is enough! Call me impatient and hard to please if you want. Condemn me as judgmental if you must, but listen to what greeted me when I opened the door and then tell me how you would have felt:

- The smell of cigarette smoke precedes him through the door. So much for his plan to quit.
- He is wearing a wrinkled, crushed velvet tan shirt that screams the seventies, is stained with coffee and looks like he just pulled it from his clothes hamper.
- He presents me a limp yellow daisy pulled from his yard, roots and all, wrapped in a wet paper towel.
- And lastly, held high next to his somewhat goofy smile he proudly displays a jug of sweet tea from Food Lion with a 69 cents sticker on it, buy one get one free!

"Oh my goodness," I thought, "this is going to be one short night!!!!!"

As I prepared to serve the meal he wondered aloud why the sherbet is being served first. Maybe it's too much to think he'd know it's to neutralize the palette. I let the matter go, but he keeps it up. "Pretty strange," he says, "dessert being served first; where I come from we always had dessert afterwards." As he is palming his wine glass in his fist and taking his first bite, I am settling into my chair. He rapidly devours his meal as if it was his last and in my book it was—at least at my address. I will admit he was apprecia-

NEXT!!

tive. The conversation continued on the couch, thankfully with the presence of my beautiful one-hundred pound black lab between us.

I know, or I fear, that sometimes as I tell these stories I might come off as snooty, someone who looks down on people. I'm not; I'm just a regular Italian girl from a decent family who worked hard to make something of herself. And I promise I never tried to humiliate or look down my nose at any of my dates. I was always kind and polite. I never let it show that I was seeking something more than they had to offer. But nights like that one helped me understand how it must feel to be a major league ballplayer sent down to the minors. One day you're flying first class between big league cities; then suddenly you're on a beat-up team bus bouncing from game to game across the Alabama countryside.

Lounging on the couch, my date says he's thrilled to be in Florida and delighted to be starting a new job that will pay eight dollars an hour! And after six months, if he is lucky, he'll go to eight-fifty. I begin talking of my health (heaven knows why) and he responds with surprise that a woman can't have a baby after a hysterectomy. He flashes that big down home grin and hopes my hot flashes will be over in a year because he'll surely be ready to spend money on a woman then.

The night was young but I was getting older by the moment, so I abruptly walked him to the door and said my family would be in tomorrow and I must rest.

He thanked me and handed me a signed lotto ticket with a chance to win five times. He says, "Angie you know I don't have a computer."

"Yes I know."

"Would you mind checking these numbers on your computer and let me know if I have any wins? I promise I will make good for you." I agree, followed by a quick cheek-to-cheek, and with a sigh he is safely on the other side of the door. As I go to dispose of the now totally dead daisy I hear the doorbell ring. There he is again. "Angie, thanks again," he says, "but may I have the rest of the sweet tea?"

Humor is a wonderful thing and that night it helped me to finally find sleep—that is after he stopped calling me to find out if we won any money on the lotto ticket. **NEXT!!**

Good point: After that evening, everyone I meet seems a little smarter.

Angie's Lessons Learned ...
Put match making on the list of things **NOT** to let family members handle for you.

"Just remember that inside every older person is a young person wondering what the hell happened."
~ Anonymous

"Sex at age 90 is like trying to shoot pool with a rope."
~ Camille Paglia, American author and social critic

THE SEASONED GENTLEMAN

Working in the skin care business specializing in age management you become well versed in how the body ages. Unfortunately the process accelerates as we grow older. For example we age faster from sixty to seventy than we do from forty to fifty. Not fair, but true.

One of my favorite brothers-in-law decided I should meet this gently seasoned gentleman who they think is maybe sixty-one. Well sixty-one and sixty-nine are very different—especially when you have been smoking for fifty years. Trusting my brother-in-law (apparently I hadn't learned my lesson from Cousin Kathy), I allowed him to give "The Seasoned Gentleman" my phone number. I would venture a guess that any of the "girlfriends" reading this chapter who

NEXT!!

have any experience at all meeting men from internet sites know the sinking feeling of believing you are meeting a peer when in fact you are about to find out that an undated picture and fudged birth date will soon bring you face-to-face with your ... grandfather! Arrgghhhh!

In this case it wasn't an internet lie that betrayed me but that tendency shared by both men and women to be too generous in assessing our own gender. It's not that we're blind, or ignorant of what makes one attractive; it's more like self-serving wish fulfillment. If I define my co-worker as "pretty," when I know she's not quite as good looking as me, then I must really be hot! Goes the same with men. If you want to know if someone is attractive, you simply have to ask a person of the opposite sex. Simple as that, which I know doesn't account for Cousin Kathy's endorsement of my previous suitor. I'm still trying to figure that one out.

> He spoke freely of the many remedies he had tried, to make things happen for him again "below the belt."

Back to my date: the seasoned gentleman is on his way to my house and I've spent nearly two hours making sure that I'm looking my best. Once again I'm dealing with a guy who—I've been told—is going to quit smoking "real soon" and, gullible as I was at the time, I actually believed it.

When I look back now I can barely comprehend how often and how easily I gave my dates the benefit of the doubt. Sometimes I suppose you really want to believe and as they say, "no pain, no gain." I know I already mentioned being lonely—maybe neurotically so—and I just hated being the brunette stuck at home on Saturday night while all the blondes were out having fun.

So the door bell rings and he's right on time. A good trait,

Angela LaTorre

I'm thinking. Wearing a friendly smile, I swing open the door. I'm greeted with lovely flowers, a shocking blue windbreaker and a face that actually made my grandfather look young.

The irony here is that I truly did enjoy my evening. The seasoned gentleman was proof that even when hopes for an ongoing romantic relationship are dashed, you can still at least have one nice night out. All and all I must admit he was an admirable gentleman and he boosted my ego, which at that point really needed it. "Boy, this is my lucky night," he said, as I locked the front door behind us. "I just picked up my new *Chrysler* and I can't wait to take you for a ride after dinner and ... would you please kiss me." He was sweet and I didn't mind.

Later he spoke freely of all the remedies he'd tried to make things happen for him again as far as ... you know ... below the belt. Nothing was working. He was gentleman enough not to say he had hoped I'd be the cure. I was able to relax, laugh and just have a great time with the seasoned gentleman. Many of the younger men I've dated could learn a lot from him.

By the way, the new *Chrysler* already reeked of smoke. I guess there was a time when most people smoked, thanks to cigarette companies handing them out free to our World War II soldiers. But those days are gone, and most of us who don't smoke don't like the odor. So if you do smoke at least take it outside. That "new car" smell won't last long if you light up and puff away. And that woman you hope to impress won't be. As for the seasoned gent, at least he remembered the strong mints and the hug good night really was sweet.

Good points: Even though there was snow on the roof he was still trying to get the fireplace burning. I hope I'm still

NEXT!!

trying when I'm his age! With no malice in my heart, I have no choice but to say, **NEXT!!**

Angie's Lessons Learned ...

Men are like gourmet cooking: A little bit of seasoning goes a long way.

> *"Cruelty is one fashion statement we can all do without."*
> ~ Rue McClanahan, American actress
>
> *"Fashion is a form of ugliness so intolerable that we have to alter it every six months."*
> ~ Oscar Wilde, Irish playwright

ELVIS HAS LEFT THE BUILDING

I often wonder what statement a man thinks he's making with a shirt worn half open to reveal a hairy chest adorned with heavy gold chains. I guess on some men it's sexy. This one coupled the gold with shoe-polished black hair and double-knit polyester pants from the early eighties. I was taking a drink from my bottled water when I first spotted him across the dance floor and with that description of him you'd think I would have broken out laughing, unable to avoid spewing water all over. Wrong! I smiled at him and waited for him to come ask me to dance—which once again shows how I was believing almost anyone could be someone special. After two nights of dancing, I agreed to a date.

Let me explain this post-divorce desperation thing a little further. You might think you can go through divorce in a nice

NEXT!!

controlled fashion but it rarely happens. Ever seen a balloon suddenly lose all its air? It goes flying around without any pattern, first one way, then the other, until all the air is gone and it's just a limp piece of latex laying empty on the floor. If someone walks up and says, "I bet you'd be beautiful if you were full of air again," it doesn't really matter if he's wearing double-knit polyester.

He was pretty good at puffing me up and was determined we would be a great couple. He was quite the dancer. I enjoyed dancing with him on several occasions before our ill-fated date.

> Have you ever noticed how in good times people make allowances for each other, but when things go bad nothing is good enough?

He offered to pick me up one Sunday afternoon in early spring to enjoy one of the complimentary floating casinos that sail from several of Florida's Atlantic ports. The morning was beautiful and I waited hopefully for him, thinking that surely his attire would be a little more casual and not so Elvis, which might be unfair to Elvis. Allow me to clarify: I should say, not so Elvis impersonator—bad Elvis impersonator.

He's an hour late and I'm thinking he must be very lost because he really does have a thing for me and would never stand me up. The phone rings. He's obviously a little unnerved, because he starts into a rambling story that begins with him buying me a beautiful bouquet of flowers and ends with him getting lost in his quest to find me and stopping to ask directions from a police officer parked at a *7-11* store. In the process he nervously locked the flowers and the keys in his running car. Needless to say we "missed the boat." When he did arrive things quickly deteriorated. Have you ever noticed how in happy times people make allowances for each other (like I did with the way he dressed), but when things go bad all of a sudden nothing about the other person is good enough? You may recognize this shifting scenario; it's often called marriage and divorce.

Well, Elvis's short visit came to an abrupt end with conversation regarding the fact that I am just a little too chubby for him and, by the way, my dancing leaves much to be desired and is **not** in the same class with his. **NEXT!!** As I watched him walk away from my door I wanted to shout something about how wrong he was to think himself fashionable in his open-throated powder blue polyester shirt with bent collar stays. I wanted to thank him for saving me a trip to the wardrobe museum, but I consoled myself with knowing that "Elvis" had left the building, never to return.

Good points: I don't have any good points for Elvis—not after he called me chubby.

Angie's Lessons Learned ...
Knockoffs and imitations may please for a while but they seldom last.

"Love begins with a smile, grows with a kiss, and ends with a teardrop."
~ Anonymous

"Ever has it been that love knows not its own depth until the hour of separation."
~ Kahlil Gibran, Lebanese-American writer

THE ONE THAT GOT AWAY

At times life can be so amazing that you think you're dreaming even when you know you're not. Then the moment ends and leaves you feeling it really was a dream after all. It can be oh so confusing.

"The One That Got Away" still occupies my thoughts and will always have a special place in my heart. Our paths first crossed in December while I was attending Christmas parties. So, to say the least, this incredibly handsome six-foot-three gentleman looked amazing to me when I spotted him in his sport jacket. His rather rugged and somewhat weathered skin spelled m-a-n in every sense. His cologne made its way to me via the gentle breeze of the river, and his glistening silver hair sparkled in the gentle light of the candles at

NEXT!!

the bar. For me the attraction was so real and immediate. I have always liked tall big men; they make me feel so safe. We danced, laughed and enjoyed a few drinks together. That was the beginning.

The next night we had dinner together and enjoyed each other's company as we shared stories and talked about our lives. His gentle manners and deep voice were just so inviting and I was comfortable.

The dating continued for seven weeks and I enjoyed every minute of it. "The One That Got Away" was unlike any man I had ever dated. I was infatuated. I did everything a woman can do to show him how I was feeling. We remain friends and for a long while I kept hoping that someday things would change. But it's really true that timing is everything. At that point his life was in transition and uncertainties regarding his career and a potential move to another country clouded our future. I needed assurance, which I guess is what led him to say goodbye. In mid January we stopped seeing each other and I must admit my heart was broken.

> Ironically, the pain I felt at losing him gave me hope for the future.

There's a song called *The Second Time Around* that says love is better when you're older, "just as wonderful with both feet on the ground." Well, that's one point of view. But on the other hand, the older you are the more complicated your life has had a chance to become. The young bring more of a blank slate to the relationship, but older lovers carry enough baggage for a summer tour of Europe.

I hated what was happening, but I had no choice but to move on. My favorite word, "Next," felt more real to me—and painful—than ever. My darling, 29-year-old son, who has wonderful wisdom said, "Mom the odds were against you; after all the ones you've dumped it was time for you to get dumped." Don't you just love your kids when they get to the age when they know more than you do? I will always cherish and appreciate the great memories I had with this gentleman and I'll always wish him well. Ladies, I hope that someday you will be able to enjoy a man like him that enjoys fine wine, has social graces, stands up when you enter the room, pulls your seat out, opens every door, waits for you to take the first bite, prays before partaking and would never think of coming to your home empty-handed. The flowers, the wine, the hot chocolate, the surf, the wind, and laughter as he serenaded me with old Dean Martin songs on our last date will forever be in my heart.

Ironically, the pain I felt at losing him became the bedrock of my hope for the future. Whenever I've had moments of despair and felt that "mister right" simply doesn't exist, I remind myself of the great times with "The One That Got Away" and am instantly blessed and acquire new hope.

Good points: Too many to mention, but I guess more than anything it was that he acted as if I was so precious that nothing he could do to make me happy was asking too much. At the time of this writing we remain good friends and I feel in my heart that we always will. Unfortunately, "NEXT" came calling and I was forced to move on.

Angie's Lessons Learned ...
Sometimes, try as you may, circumstances are beyond your control.

"It is always good policy to tell the truth unless of course you are an exceptionally good liar."
~ Jerome K. Jerome, English humorist

THE BIKER

As many of you may know, the Daytona Beach area is famous for racing and that includes motorcycles. The area hosts two motorcycle events each year: *"Biketoberfest"* in October and *"Bike Week"* in February. Both events offer tourists from colder climates a chance to let loose in the Florida sun. These events are not primarily about racing. They are about cruising, styling and partying as the bikers ride from one biker-friendly watering hole to another.

On a Tuesday evening during October at a local venue in Ormond Beach called *"The Rockin' Ranch"* a group of us met to dance. Of course the scene was a buzz of bikers galore. "The Biker," is smiling and looking rather interested and then takes the quite common initiative of buying me a drink. I look over to thank him and he approaches. He's another big boy but this one apparently has a big wallet to go with his two-hundred and sixty pound body, which is creatively distributed on a six-foot-two frame. At least he made it seem the wallet was never ending. He had that big teddy bear look about him but was very fair, blue-eyed and so well outfitted in everything Harley Davidson has to offer.

 He quickly announced that he was single and thinking about relocating to the Daytona area after he retires next year. He has made his millions and just loves everything about Daytona, Ormond and all the beach towns that comprise our county. All of this sounded so good to me. Of course, these are very convenient words for a man who wants more. Having been born and raised in the Northern part of Pennsylvania and now fifty-one years old he is ready for a change. He explained that his 26-year-old son is ready to take over the business and handle the family fortune so daddy can move on with his life, and take off on his big Harley—a bike that had been cross country several times— and continue riding off into the sunset.

> When married men are away from home, the temptation to play around is very real.

 Like "The One That Got Away," The Biker had that gentle giant way about him that is just so appealing and so hard to resist.

 But of course there is always more to the story. Just like older gentlemen with money who use it to capture the perfect woman, usually fifteen to twenty years younger, the "capture" is only the opening chapter. As I said, there's always more to the story. The problem with such wishful and shallow scenarios is they usually backfire in the long run because there is so much more to life than the packaging. I recently spoke to a ladies Christian group called "The Woman's Connection" regarding age management. After the meeting the motivational speaker chatted with me and said, "Angie, sometimes God has a beautiful gift he wants to present to you as a potential companion and we often are so consumed with the packaging, which may be a common paper bag, that we never allow ourselves to open it and see the real value inside."

Well, so much for the wisdom of hindsight. All in all at that moment "The Biker" was more than appealing and he was here for a week. So I picked out a tee shirt from one of the many *Biketoberfest* vendors, put on his extra helmet, mounted his comfortable ride, and we were off. The hundred dollar bills were stacked and to my amazement he went through them like I do dimes. We had a great time, expensive dinners, fun friends, scenic rides, great music and a fresh rose every time we stopped for gas. It was a bit like a romantic movie, I must admit. He drank more root beer than beer so I always felt safe. We laughed, shared notes about our grandkids and then, sadly, he was off to return to his responsibilities in Pennsylvania. He left me with warm feelings toward him. Even though I wasn't sure where things would go with him, I was feeling that after so many dating catastrophes I was finally doing something right.

As the weeks passed, we stayed in contact and had great conversations. But I instantly saw a pattern unfold that consisted of my being allowed to call him at work only, never at home. Sound familiar? Over the course of about two months it became obvious to me that there was more to this story. I am reminded time and time again of Dr. Phil's words, "Listen to what they are *not* telling you." Listen with a capital **L**. I soon realized his words were just too wonderful and so easy when the wife is stashed miles away. A lesson learned: When married men are away from home, the temptation to play around is very real. Our contact soon ended when I told him, "I've got your number and by the way it's not your home phone number." He confessed and I expressed my

NEXT!!

disappointment and of course strong disapproval, having myself experienced the pain of a cheating spouse.

Good points: The riding was fun and I don't regret the experience. But he was very definitely a **NEXT!!** No married men, please!

Angie's Lessons Learned ...
Be aware of your own desires and weaknesses, and you'll avoid being an easy mark.

"The true hypocrite is the one who ceases to perceive his deception, the one who lies with sincerity."
~ Andre Gide, French author

"As I speak now, a scam is being born."
~ Jane Feather, Romance novelist

THE SCAM ARTIST

There is a big difference between the "ballroom" and the "bar room" as far as the dance community. Unfortunately in a small town the ballroom is not always accessible. In the bar room situation you are liable to meet gentlemen with stories, plans and baggage galore. As far as baggage goes, it's hard to avoid completely, but I've learned the hard way that there's a vast difference between having baggage enough to fill a small duffle bag as compared to the entire *Samsonite* set.

"The Scam Artist" was young, as in forty-two, buff and way too handsome. That should have been a red flag from the beginning but remember I was newly divorced and very inexperienced. Maybe by this time you think I should have been wising up a little, but I started out pretty naïve and, as

NEXT!!

I said, he was very buff and handsome. I was easy prey.

My handsome younger man smiled, came over and began a conversation in between songs. He was a county law enforcement officer. My first thought was, good, he has to be clean as far as not having a record and surely he is very law abiding. The "not having a record" part was true, but he'd put together a clever scam that, I learned later, he'd worked on other women before me. I was his latest scam target. In my case it was mainly a great attempt. You could say I got off cheap.

He walked me to my car and very slowly looked over the entire vehicle especially the license tag. I had no idea at the time what his mission was. The next day I found flowers and a lovely card on my front step. I never gave him my address or phone number. On the card was his phone number. Mission accomplished. He had my phone number, called and we agreed to meet for lunch on our first date. He said he was single after two divorces, which should have been another red flag for a man so young.

> Maybe it was the easy way he took me in, and partly his good looks, but I couldn't let it go.

His personality was warm and fun and his looks were amazing. He obviously spent a considerable amount of time at the gym and he was somewhat of a natural pretty boy. Along with the lunch came a stack of photo albums and his life story. Of course the stories went hand-in-hand with the photos and there was a lot of "poor me" and a heavy past. He was conceived out of wedlock and when he met his biological siblings for the first time at his real father's funeral a fight broke out and he was rejected. His second wife left him for a "man of God" and she had been ordained as a minister herself. My handsome scam artist explained how he worked very long hours in an effort to keep his eighteen and seventeen-year-old sons in shoes and food. On and on the stories mounted. Any moment I expected a violin player to appear next to our table. I wondered if I'd hear how as a boy he had to walk ten miles to school each day—in the snow, with holes in his shoes and uphill both ways. Would he say he had to beg other kids for a bite or two of their lunch? My appetite grew weaker and weaker.

Our second and last date was on a Friday night. He had called and asked me out and as we were driving to a casual Greek restaurant, he confessed that he had no money until his next paycheck. His last bi-monthly paycheck went to keeping a roof over his children's heads and his car payment. The generous woman that I am, of course I offered to take care of dinner. I love Greek food and this was Daytona's finest. We sat on the balcony overlooking lovely downtown Daytona Beach with a spectacular view of the Halifax River. The torches were lit, the wine was fine and the breeze was perfect. His face was like that of a chiseled sculpture I remembered seeing in Rome. I drank him in with my eyes as we enjoyed some great espresso and sweeter than sweet Baklava.

But my evening was suddenly ruined when he expressed concern for his two boys who were home and hungry because his clergy-woman ex-wife hadn't come through with the $100 she owed for child support that week. Apparently the offering at her church was a little down. No disrespect to the church or the clergy but I was totally turned off by the whole situation. On our way to the supermarket to buy food for the boys I thought to myself, "here we go again; another Next!" And I was finally starting to ask myself, "What is going on out there in this world of the single life?"

After meeting his two delightful sons and watching them

NEXT!!

devour food as if they hadn't had a good meal in days, I decided to say "goodbye." I felt a bit used, but like a Good Samaritan at the same time.

Maybe it was the easy way he took me in, and partly his good looks, but I couldn't just forget it. With a little research I concluded that on the night we met he took my license tag number so he could use the data base at work to find out everything about me, not only my address but everything I owned, etc. etc. He was a "Scam Artist." The photos, flowers, charm and sob story were all a plan to try and find a woman to help support him. He was one beautiful man with a failed plan!

Ironically, six months later I was happy to acquire a new client in the salon who turned out to be a true "sister." She was of Latin descent and a lawyer just beginning her practice in our county. She was about my age and was recently divorced as well. As I gently massaged and treated her beautiful skin we began to talk girl-to-girl regarding the single life and the obstacles for women like us. She said, "Yes, you have to be careful," and mentioned meeting a man who presented himself in such a charming way and described how their first date consisted of lunch and the photo album session.

You can bet my ears perked up! After additional comments and matching our stories, we were stunned to conclude we had both been scammed by the same man! Because of her legal background and having a few more years experience with single life, she avoided the second date. We laughed and wanted to cry at the same time; it was too coincidental and very amazing.

By that point "The Scam Artist" had already been tossed on my fast-growing **NEXT!!** pile, but it was nice to learn my instincts had been right.

Good points: I enjoyed watching his hungry sons eat hearty, and I slept with the heart of a Good Samaritan that night. I truly believe when you follow your heart, God will reward you in the end.

Angie's Lessons Learned ...
Once again it was proven: If it seems too good to be true, it probably is.

"There is hope for any woman who can look in a mirror and laugh at what she sees"
~ Anonymous

FACING MYSELF

You might wonder why a chapter titled "Facing Myself" would come so far into my story, but I believe that's the way it usually happens. In my quest to reestablish my life as a single woman, learn how to manage my career, make good choices and handle my finances, I found myself in the midst of some tricky career decisions which finally led me to look hard in the mirror. Not that all my decisions about men suddenly became wise decisions—you'll soon see that didn't happen—but at least I understood myself a little better.

For reasons beyond my control, my days as an independent medical aesthetician working with an amazing plastic surgeon were coming to an end. I was compelled to make a move. I entertained the idea of moving south to start my life over in an area that housed no memories of my thirty-year marriage. An opportunity soon presented itself. I'd be part

NEXT!!

of a great team with a growing company involving pharmaceutical sales with a product line I already was familiar with. The South Florida territory was mine and I would be closer to my two beautiful grandsons and my son and daughter-in-law.

While in this transition mode I was blessed to spend the warm summer month of August with my mother and stepfather. I can't think about my mother without realizing how blessed I am, but to say the least, it was interesting to live at home again at age fifty-one. Believe it or not, my mother's house rules reverted all the way back to the days before my marriage. She even gave me a curfew! I kid you not, 11 p.m. on weekdays and midnight on the weekend. If I'd been going to school I think she would have dug out my old *Barbie* lunch box.

> She shared with me that peace is the most important thing when you are single. I never forgot her. And I never accused myself of being a quitter.

It was a laughably memorable month but my love for my mother grew. It reminded me of the time we spent together when she carried out my Dad's life-long dream of taking his entire family to Italy. In 2004, the year before my divorce, eighteen of us enjoyed that dream with my mother. Those were the best eighteen days of my life and it was while traveling in Italy that I confirmed to myself what I already suspected: I could not stay in my marriage.

Italy is indescribably beautiful. Its splendor cannot be put in words or illustrated, it must be witnessed and felt in the soul. I'm not sure if it was the contrast with Italy's beauty that finally caused me to see the sour face my marriage had taken on. Maybe it was the wide gulf between the invigorating joy of our trip and the sorry boredom of my marriage, but I knew then I had to have more. I believe every failed marriage has such a moment when one or both partners know it's over. The lucky ones, the ones truly meant for each other, see the moment coming before it's too late.

But for most of us it's a Humpty-Dumpty tale. One moment you're sitting high on the wall that separates you from the uncertainty of single life. The next moment you've lost your balance and your marriage has crashed and broken into a million pieces that all the king's horses and all the king's men can't reassemble. While in Italy I knew my days on the wall would soon be over. I've thought once or twice about finding a picture book to see if Humpty-Dumpty was smiling on his way down. I know I was. Then of course comes the moment of impact. That's when the pain begins.

I turned fifty-two on August 31st. My family had a big birthday and good luck celebration as I was off the very next day to venture down new avenues in my life. My small car was jam-packed with the essentials of life and I was fearfully uncertain of where I was going and what I was doing. The only peace I had at that time was the peace and love of my family. That peace bears no price, is not tangible and is beyond words. Without my family I would not be here telling you my story.

I arrived in Singer Island, just east of North Palm Beach. The condo I had rented in advance was ill-kept, poorly furnished and in need of intense cleaning. I battled fear and depression but reminded myself that I'm a survivor and too strong to be beaten (sometimes you have to lie to yourself!). I was determined to make due for a month and to make a go of my new business opportunity. I reference the peace my family's love gave me because during that twenty-three day period I struggled to feel any peace. Everything went wrong even to the point of scary intruders. South Florida is a differ-

NEXT!!

ent world and after much experience I will opt to live and enjoy the wonders and peace of Central Florida's Atlantic Coast any time. People who know me think I'm a pretty tough cookie, but underneath I sometimes feel like that little girl carrying a *Barbie* lunch box, thankful "Mommy" is there to put up boundaries. At the risk of selling short my sisters, I often think feeling safe in a marriage is what makes many women continue to tolerate demeaning comments and toilet seats left in the upright position long after the affection is gone.

Everything I touched in South Florida went sour. Most housing was unaffordable, except in neighborhoods of questionable safety. The potential business leads proved unfruitful. The company's many promises were not in writing and their memories of our previous conversations differed vastly from mine. In the grip of all this madness I was terribly homesick. My clients, some of whom I'd served for twenty years, were calling me. "Where are you?" they would ask. "My face needs you!"

It was nice to feel needed and on September 20, 2007, which would have been my thirty-second wedding anniversary, as I was swimming in the pool and trying to delude myself about my personal strength, I decided, "I am going back home."

I quickly packed up my essentials, instantly feeling my spirit and determination beginning to soar, and started back north to regain my peace. On the way home I reflected for a time on a woman I met at a local gym who had been divorced for ten years after a long marriage. She shared with me that peace is the most important thing when you are single. I never forgot her. And I never accused myself of being a quitter.

Good points: I came out of this testing time knowing my

strengths and weaknesses, and no longer feeling I needed to respond to my ex-husband's persistent taunting that I couldn't make it on my own. I could accept my limitations, succeed in my own way, be myself and be proud of the woman I am.

Angie's Lessons Learned ...
Never let someone else determine the measure of your success in life.

"I feel sorry for people who don't drink. When they wake up in the morning, that's as good as they're going to feel all day."
~ Frank Sinatra

THE ALCOHOLIC

On September 23rd after staying two nights with a girlfriend to whom I will always be grateful, I set out to find a place to rent in beautiful New Smyrna Beach, a somewhat sleepy beach town nestled between the waters of Ponce Inlet and the Canaveral Shoreline. For many years this charming town, where change has come slowly, has been one of Florida's best kept secrets.

Nearly exhausted from a long day searching for a short-term rental, I stumbled across a condo with an affordable efficiency unit. It would become my home for five months and it was there I met "The Alcoholic." He happened to live down the hall from my two hundred square foot efficiency and before I learned of his struggles with alcohol I thought he could be a prospect for the future.

Before I tell you of his wonders, let me entertain you with the joys of living in an efficiency. For various reasons I never

NEXT!!

experienced the college scene and "dorm life." I suppose that at age fifty-one it was finally my turn. I've always been one to look for the bright side of a situation and find the silver lining. Those five months were extremely challenging, to say the least, but not without rewards. For the first time in my life I was able to lie in bed and feel the fragrant beachside breeze of the Atlantic Ocean just steps away, view a bit of the sunrise, see my kitchen, see my bathroom vanity, enjoy the reflections of the lights on the condo swimming pool below, and control TV, video and stereo systems without ever moving. How efficient is that? Until then I had never considered why little studio apartments are called "efficiencies." Everything a woman could want in one small space, if the woman's wants aren't measured in large quantities.

> This handsome man was a prime example of one who looked to temporarily drown his pain instead of eliminating it. He should have been in his glory ...

But one of my favorite holiday memories came in that little condo. That most joyous occasion was the one and only Christmas night that my then one-year-old grandson, Matthew, spent the night with his "Nona." It had been a long, fun filled Christmas Day with my big Sicilian family. By midnight the kid was finally beat. "Matthew, time to go night-night," I said. With his soft blanket and "Winnie the Pooh" book tightly clasped in his hands, he looked around for where he would sleep. His eyes fell on Nona's bed. (You couldn't miss it right in the middle of that little room!) He watched with an inquisitive eye as I walked to the wall and dimmed the lonely light above where he would sleep. But where? To see the look of amazement on his face, you would have thought he'd witnessed a great magic trick as the Murphy bed began to descend from the wall. He proceeded to climb up onto the bed and looked up and around with a face totally exhausted from the day's events, but in pure bliss. "Wow Nona, wow," he repeated, "night, night." It was at that moment that I realized once again that the best things in life are truly free and that moment carried me through the rest of my time there.

Back to my neighbor down the hall: Words fail for explaining the immediate attraction, but I don't think I was the first woman to experience it. Forty-three years old, six-foot, nicely built, and with a face that would make Pierce Brosnan envious. His smile would light up his eyes and makes those deep dimples even more exciting. His sparkling salt and pepper hair and the gentle waves completed "the look." This was a very handsome man—and younger than me. Of course I was drawn in!

We exchanged smiles and an initial hello and at the end of that first conversation he asked, "Where are you off to?" It wasn't long before we became friends and I immediately became very fond of his nine-year-old daughter who would visit bimonthly. But I soon discovered his not-so-handsome side. For all his goodness and having his heart in the right place, he had a major problem. He too frequently sought refuge from his pain with alcohol. I immediately felt somewhat compelled to save him and did on many occasions, going out in the wee hours of the morning to bring him home safely.

A past full of challenges and a few too many bad decisions along the way paved the way for a submerged anger that would surface when his thoughts of regret combined with any form of alcohol. Of course many people go through times of trial without giving in to alcohol, drug abuse or other self-destructive behavior. I'm not a doctor, but I've seen

NEXT!!

my share of life, and I believe times of change—like a divorce—can make us vulnerable to threats we might withstand in more secure times. If you are in such a time, as I was, be on the alert. Seek help if you need it.

This handsome man was a prime example of one who looked to temporarily drown his pain instead of eliminating it. He should have been in his glory; his incredible and highly intelligent daughter was blooming into a young woman and many of the issues he had faced were not his fault. He had no reason to feel guilt and regardless of his troubles he was a pure delight with a personality like no other person I had ever met. Together we had a great time.

When I think of him, I remember my admiration for him above the sadness of his alcoholism. He had a father's love for his child that was unconditional, and to watch this man bundle that with amazing child-rearing skills was a blessing. His daughter was, and still is, beautiful, precious, smart, witty, incredibly modest and very appreciative—on her way to becoming a magnetically charming young woman.

I have learned many lessons from this great friend and his daughter, including not to judge people based on their flaws alone. We are all complex beings and deserve credit where it's due, no matter our failings.

We enjoyed some great times, especially in the sky. I didn't mention that he is a fine pilot as well. I flew with him many times but never when he was drinking! I will always cherish our friendship. I've learned to treat life a little like a treasure hunt. Sometimes objects of great value are hidden where you'd least expect to find them.

Good points: We will always be friends. I say **NEXT!** reluctantly. I hope some day he will be blessed with a woman who is worthy of his heart and gentle ways. But I doubt that wish will come true for him until he learns to face himself just as I was forced to do. That's my first wish for him, that he will some day come to accept himself and overcome his alcoholism.

Angie's Lessons Learned ...
You can't "fix" another person, you can only show them that you care.

"Jealousy is the tie that binds, and binds, and binds."
~ Helen Rowland, American Humorist

"Jealousy is the only vice that gives no pleasure."
~ Anonymous

THE JEALOUS ONE

Being a bit of a dedicated ballroom dancer with a desire to become even better I try to go dancing at least a few times a week. I mentioned earlier that the ballroom and bar room are not to be confused. They are totally different scenes. There's also a third dance venue which every now and again I decide to visit: singles dances. I think I've already described for you twelve, maybe fifteen, failed attempts to find my "Mr. Right." At that point some women might whine and cry, "I'm just going to give up. Who needs a man to be fulfilled anyway!" That's not my style. I asked myself, "What's wrong with one more try?"

From across the room I spot what appears to be a nicely dressed man, mid-fifties with a very appealing smile. He spotted me spotting him and he apparently felt the same

NEXT!!

way about my smile. Within minutes he had crossed the floor and asked me to dance. He was nice, lived in the Orlando area and had no visible tattoos, piercing or hanging objects, and seemed to be a professional man. I was fairly attracted to him and decided, after talking and dancing with him, to give him my phone number when he asked for it. He said he had his own business, didn't live with Momma, was taller and not prettier than me, so why not? He had met the minimum standard requirements, and I was single and feeling rather free. We danced, chatted and were collectively planning our next possible visit together. We enjoyed two dates, both meeting in public places. He seemed very nice and I agreed to visit him at his home because I was not comfortable at this early stage with him coming to my home. Although he presented himself as an independent successful business owner his small garage apartment over a one-car garage depicted something else.

I patiently waited in the rather tiny living room as he dressed for our third date. Much to my surprise, without warning, I heard a loud insistent pounding at his front door just inches from my ears. The ex-girlfriend was strangely enough an "ex" in his mind only, not in hers. She had called earlier and left word that she would be in the neighborhood and would be stopping by. My date, I learned later, decided to ignore that message but she was not about to ignore the fact that there was a strange car in his driveway—namely mine! After what seemed to be endless minutes of banging and yelling his name through the door—along with a few choice words—she left but not for long. She moved her car, quietly snuck back and walked undetected up the outside stairs. When we opened the door to leave, surprise, surprise, there she was! My date was well acquainted with her game and it soon became apparent to me this was not the first time they'd played this scene. It was also apparent to me that he was a bit of a player/liar. He was obviously in somewhat of a committed relationship with her but wanted a little extra fun on the side. The irate girlfriend left but I was more than uncomfortable and asked him to escort me to my car to make sure the coast was clear.

This is going to be another one of those points when you say, "What the heck were you thinking Angie," but at his insistence I agreed to follow him to dinner, listen to his pitiful explanation and then hand him his walking papers. Once again, I was pretty new to this whole dating scene and more naïve than I am now. And truthfully, I didn't understand codependency. Eventually he'd reveal that she wasn't the only one possessed by the green-eyed monster. But that night he presented what sounded like a valid explanation, and then turned on the charm machine. We ended up having a nice evening. He was incredibly respectful and quite the gentleman.

Two months went by and we continued seeing each other. There were flowers, cards, surprise invitation dates to lunch, and nice gifts. He had a lovely daughter and I took that as evidence he was OK. Things were good. After the ninety-day rule period had passed and the possibility arose of things moving to the next level, he invited me to go away with him for Memorial Day Weekend. I agreed.

I was living in a town home that needed some minor repairs and he was quite the "Mr. Fixit." He also was very concerned about my security. On that premise he said he'd come over the day before our trip, while I was working, and take care of the "honey do list." I was impressed and grateful. At 5:15 that evening dinner was on the table and the list was complete except for installing a pin to secure the large sliding glass door. He looked at me and said, "We're gonna

NEXT!!

need to break out the heavy artillery for this job."

"Well I wondered how you were going to install that pin. The metal on the doors looks pretty thick."

He snapped open a molded plastic case and held up what looked to me like a normal power drill. His voice seemed to get deeper as he spoke.

"I hold in my hand the *DeWalt* 18-volt hammer drill, the most powerful hand tool known to man. It will penetrate anything—metal, concrete, you name it."

I was thinking of that Dirty Harry scene where Clint Eastwood warns the bad guy, you're looking down the barrel of the most powerful handgun known to man. "Well," I said, "don't point that thing at little ol' me."

"Sorry ma'am," he said. "I'll just install this metal-eating drill bit and get to work."

What is it about men and their power tools? Somehow it seems to bring out the primitive masculinity in them, like in the Tim Allen television show *Home Improvement,* where his manly "call of the wild" was always *More Power!* "The Jealous One" continued to talk as he worked, describing the job to me as he went along, and I swear his voice dropped down an octave lower.

I don't see it as a bad trait in a man that he wants to be protective of the woman in his life, and I could see his pride growing as he finished the job, knowing he was adding to my sense of security.

"That's it," he said, testing how the pin fit in the hole he'd drilled. "Nice and snug. No way anyone's breaking in here now." There was a little chain that attached the pin to the door so it would hang there when not in use. "I'll just drill this self-tapping screw into the door frame to attach the chain, and we'll be clear to leave for our weekend, knowing things are good and safe here," he said.

Angela LaTorre

I really did appreciate his help, and stepped close to him to say so, resting my hand on his arm as I gave him a little kiss on the cheek. His face turned red as I smiled at him. He was lost for words. He was still holding the steel pin in his hand and for some reason he tossed it high in the air in front of him. But it didn't stay in front of him. We both looked up, watching it rotate end over end, as if in slow motion. It looked like it was going to come down and hit him on the head. He leaned back like a kid at the ballpark, putting his hands up to make the catch. And like the kid at the park, he muffed it. The pin bounced off his hands and hit the sliding glass door hard, shattering it in a billion pieces.

What a mess and what an embarrassment to him. Of course, it is the Friday before Memorial Day and it's now 8 o'clock in the evening. Our plans are suddenly on hold. Taping up a heavy piece of plastic might keep out the rain but certainly not a burglar. But he got lucky (with finding a repairman). After numerous phone calls he was successful in hiring someone who could come and replace the glass Saturday morning. Total price tag: $580. But my friend kept his spirits up, enjoyed his night on the couch downstairs, and was anxious to start our weekend after writing out the check.

> No woman should feel bullied, intimidated or threatened by a man. And a man who tries that tactic needs to be taught that it's wrong.

Finally, we were off to a nice destination two hours south, a large bed and breakfast that bordered on being an inn. The sun was shining, he was smiling, and of course planning the next step as far as getting lucky—this time not with the repairman. There is so much to be said about taking a lot of time to really get to know someone and experiencing many

NEXT!!

aspects of their life. Well, thirty minutes of experience on I-95 began to give me second thoughts and had me wishing I'd brought my own car. His road rage was thundering, coupled with wild speeding and horrible language. I have more tolerance for irate ex-girlfriends than for words from the gutter. I was not happy, but he was high on an emotional thrill ride and seemed rather proud of his behavior. My expectations were sinking fast and the word NEXT! kept racing through my mind.

Then we arrived. I tried to calm down and just enjoy a weekend away. The bed and breakfast was friendly and comfortable, and I heard him call his daughter to tell her how wonderful everything was and how he loved being with me. But it was just a momentary plateau on our downhill slide. As we dressed for dinner, a conversation began regarding my dancing and how he didn't like me going on weekend dance events and staying overnight and on and on. This kind of behavior began shortly after we first met. He knew it offended me and he often promised to be better about it. But he couldn't or wouldn't stop. Jealousy was an obvious issue for him.

We went down to the dining room and I decided to turn the tables and casually reminded him of his raging girlfriend showing up when we first met and "admitted" I wasn't sure she was truly out of the picture since they had dated for three years. That shut him up, at least for a minute. Smooth jazz was playing in the background and I tried to change the mood by pleasantly commenting on how tasty and well-prepared the appetizer was. It was true. The entire setting at the bed and breakfast was very relaxing but not relaxing enough for my jealous friend. He started up again and I countered by inviting our inn keeper, who was sitting at the bar, to come over. I knew him fairly well because I had made

Angela LaTorre

frequent trips to South Florida to visit my son and his family and the inn was half-way in between. I'd stayed there on more than one occasion. Our host was a taller Jimmy Buffet type with impeccable manners. I guess I was hoping his good manners would wear off on "the jealous one," and if not, that the inn-keeper's six-foot-four frame would intimidate my five-foot-nine friend. It sounds crass, but he was trying to intimidate me with his jealous rages.

Of course, if my date had been totally without social skills he wouldn't have reached the ninety day mark. He smiled and chatted with the inn keeper, but once our host walked away it was back to business as usual. He was becoming more and more belligerent and more intoxicated; I was becoming more and more unhappy. Let me quote his words as the main course was being served: "Well do you dance with him too and have you danced with him in bed?" At that point I was done. I had no desire to even touch his hand much less be intimate with him for the first time. He was so extremely jealous that he turned into quite the jerk.

I had taken all I was going to take. I threw down my napkin and said, "That's it, I am out of here!" Then I paused to take several bites of my delicious lobster—well, it was lobster!—and walked out.

One of my policies is to always have an escape plan and my girlfriend Dara, who lived nearby, was "Johnny on the Spot." I was packed and waiting for her within twenty minutes. Of course he was more than surprised that I was leaving him with the mandatory three-night bill due to the holiday, a large dinner bill (lobster was not exactly in season) along with the repairs to the glass door at my town home. All in all he was out about $1,800, and he never got "lucky." I didn't and don't feel guilty about it. No woman should feel bullied, intimidated or threatened by a man. And a man

NEXT!!

who tries that tactic needs to be taught that it's wrong. Maybe some future, more fortunate woman eventually benefited from my taking "The Jealous One" to school. Maybe that $1,800 could be considered tuition. But I doubt that it's tax-deductible.

I enjoyed the rest of the weekend with my old friend, renewing a sense of sisterhood. I went home, put his tools on my front porch and when he called I told him, "lose my number!"

Good points: My town home looked great, the new glass on the sliding door was glistening and once again I learned some valuable lessons with this guy. I was going through a process of elimination as to what personality traits to avoid. I had seen his jealous tendencies right away but let it go. I wouldn't do that again. Next time I see that kind of possessive jealousy, it will be **NEXT!!** right away.

Angie's Lessons Learned ...
Jealousy is neurotic behavior. It can't be wished away. It requires treatment!

*"You know we're goin' to Surf City,
gonna have some fun ..."*
~ Jan and Dean, from 1963 No. 1 hit, *Surf City*

MATCH.COM AGAIN AND THE SURFER

It had now been over three years since I last attempted the dating scenario I call "internet madness," so it was time to give it another try. I still had the classy photos sold to me by that self-described "legitimate" modeling agency which claimed to be looking for middle-aged women who are bigger than a size six. Apparently they didn't like what they saw—or were they really only in the business of selling photo portfolios? You think?

Being a woman that doesn't like waste, I decided to take a few of the nicer photos and give *Match.com* another try. What's the old English saying? "In for a penny, in for a pound?" In those days my response was usually, "Why not!"

It was early August and my stock on *Match.com* was hot as the summer sun. From August 1 to August 8 my friendly smile generated over seventeen hundred hits, mostly from within a fifty mile radius. Slowly and methodically, I canvassed the potentials. After eliminating the thirty-two year-olds, guys from states clear across the country, the ones

NEXT!!

who listed flea markets as their main idea of fun, those feeling the need to stand in front of an expensive car, or show off a well-decorated home as if I wanted to date a leather couch, I had cut down the field considerably. Then I deleted those who didn't take enough time to write or spell coherently, the muscle flexers, the old and toothless, and finally the casual posers with the baseball cap on backwards.

A week of cleaning up shrank my swelling pool of suitors down to a tiny puddle of three possibilities. I started with the retired boy wonder. He was to present himself on the second attempt after he'd called at the last minute to cancel our first potential meeting on a Sunday afternoon. Of course, I let him know he basically ruined my whole day but I decided to give him a second chance because his manners on the phone were nice and he seemed sincerely apologetic. Our rescheduled meeting was to take place in his hometown at a convenient location within five minutes of his home and close to the highway. I was traveling home from a five-day visit with the two most important men in my life, my grandsons. I made it clear to him that it would be a short "meet and greet" as I would be road weary.

> Here's the valuable lesson: Don't date a man who is newly divorced and still has a boatload of financial and bitterness issues.

So I started out ready to forgive and forget but I ended up quickly put off by a man for whom control seem to be a compulsive, almost neurotic issue. There's a fine line between leading and controlling and men tell me they're often confused about how much "leadership" women appreciate. If they say, "We're going to have dinner at 'abc' restaurant," the woman might reply that she would have appreciated being asked where she'd like to eat. But if he says, "Where do you want to eat tonight dear?" he gets treated as an indecisive momma's boy. Guys, there's an art to finding the middle ground, but you'll have to discover it on your own. Personally, what I don't like is demands. My date had clearly demanded that I meet him at the bar as he "will be ready for my first beer of the day." I've always been reluctant to sit alone at a bar so I ordered an appetizer and patiently waited in a booth facing the parking lot. I recognized his car from pictures on *Match.com*, remembering it because it's the same model as mine. I watched him enter the bar, looking several years older and many pounds larger than his online pictures.

The heat and humidity of a Florida August day had gotten the best of him and his shirt was stuck to his skin. I watched in somewhat embarrassed amazement as he stood at the bar, loosened his shorts, pulled up his shirt and let it all hang out. The hanging was plentiful. He spotted me, tucked himself back in and began to waddle toward me. He reached my booth, I said hello and he shot back with a quick and unappreciated reply: "I told you to meet me at the bar." At that point I should have said, "thanks but no thanks." However, my appetizer was coming and I was hungry. After taking a few quick bites while watching him guzzle down two beers from the largest ice tea glasses made, I paid the bill. Since he made no apology for his rude remark, I said that I had way too much going on for this to work, and left.

I started by qualifying the second of my three candidates with several phone conversations and felt pretty good about him by the time we met. We selected a nice Italian restaurant and he arrived with a lovely rose in hand. I thought, "There are some guys still out there who get it." The restaurant was pleasant, and the food was decent as he also appeared to be. However within seventeen minutes I knew all

NEXT!!

about the financial woes that surrounded his divorce, and how he doesn't understand why his five kids and ex-wife refuse to have contact with him. That was topped by a laundry list of complaints about financial issues and wayward behavior regarding minor children.

I had enjoyed the food and the rose, but not the company. The simple truth is, he wasn't ready to be good company to any woman. And here's the valuable lesson: Don't date a man who is newly divorced and still has a boatload of financial and bitterness issues.

I had started out with three *Match.com* prospects and the first two turned out to be "one date wonders." But you know all the sayings about the number three: On the positive side you have, "the third time's the charm," and of course, "good things come in threes." Then, on the other hand, you have "three strikes and you're out!" Which would it be for me, a home run or a sad walk back to the dugout?

Well, the third attempt seemed promising. He was handsome, fun and seemed to have a lot of good things going on. The problem was that his life was governed by the sea. Yes, the beautiful Atlantic Ocean in wonderful New Smyrna Beach, one of Florida's top surf spots. He would drive to New Smyrna each weekend from more than an hour away. Unfortunately, he didn't come just to see me. He had been coming even before he met me. The fact is, he was a surfer boy and no woman, no matter what her physical attributes, could ever intrigue him like a glassy set of waves rolling toward shore. I learned early on that if "the surf is firing," it didn't matter one bit whether or not I was "firing" too. Between me and the sea, the sea always took priority. Our eight-week courtship was fun and I must admit, hot. It's said that rules are meant to be broken so I'll admit ninety days is not a hard and fast rule. How many times have you heard a friend say, "When there's chemistry you know it right away." When I met the surfer I was filled immediately with a volcanic chemical reaction! I was saddened when things ended, even though in reflection it was obvious that after hours and hours of surfing to the point of exhaustion there was not enough time or energy left to satisfy me in addition to the travel time to get back home and prepare for the week.

So, good riddance to the surfer. Let him sleep with the ocean. I think maybe all that time in the surf led to "water on the brain." I don't mean to sound bitter, because when I think of him the memories are pleasant to say the least. He was in fabulous physical shape and the tan lines were amazing. I wish him all the best because he was truly a cool guy, just not a good match for me. **NEXT!!**

Good points: Even though I never felt I was his top priority, when we were together he always treated me pleasantly and didn't seem to harbor any concealed issues that would suddenly flame up.

Angie's Lessons Learned ...
On a long journey it's OK to stop off for some fun before reaching your destination.

> *"Charming people live up to the very edge of their charm, and behave as outrageously as the world lets them."*
> ~ Logan Pearsall Smith, American essayist

THE CHARMER

Well the time had come for me to meet another candidate on *Match.com* and this one needs a chapter all his own. There are apparently men out there who have some of the same motivations as women as far as finding someone with the potential to help support them. Shocking, I know. I suppose it makes me a sexist even to suggest something is wrong with that. I prefer to think of myself as a traditionalist.

I am not sure to this day if that was the case with this gentlemen, but by date number three I was beginning to wonder. After over three years of actively dating I had concluded that the third date is the one that is going to determine if we continue, or say our "goodbyes" now. Date number one, "the meet and greet," is often sweet because you are content just to see if there's any attraction, and of course you are more likely than not to be complimentary—despite

NEXT!!

what you may be thinking. Meeting number two, in my book, is mostly dedicated to what I call my "three L's" (Look, Learn and Listen). I watch how the man behaves in public and determine how generous and caring he is by the way he treats me and others—like servers in restaurants for instance.

Please understand that in time, by date number four or five, I am willing to invite him to my home, cook for him and enjoy a nice evening with a potential gentleman; I am a giver and believe in a true partnership in every respect. But if on the second date he balks at my ordering a glass of wine, then I have to wonder whether he is having financial troubles or maybe is just too frugal for my taste. He doesn't need to be extravagant, but is wanting to enjoy life a little a federal crime? That didn't apply to "The Charmer," but something about his showy, maybe deceptive, way with money got me thinking about the opposite situation.

> They say you can't judge a book by its cover and it was time to stow this charming book back on the shelf. NEXT!!

The learning part of my three L's involves listening to what he has to say about his life and looking for red flags (i.e., I don't get along with my kids or mother, haven't spoken to my father in years and my ex-wife is a real "B"). Listening carefully is important and helps me really zoom in and get a feel for what he might not be telling me (yes, if that sounds familiar, it is advice from Dr. Phil).

As we all know, there are three sides to every story—mine, yours and the truth, and we women often hear just his side as far as the ex-wife (or wives) goes. I have often thought it would be great to look up all these ex-wives. Wouldn't it be fun to hear their side? In my opinion, a divorced man—or woman—should say as little as possible about their ex, and keep it short and positive. For example: "There were some wonderful things about her or I wouldn't have married her. Unfortunately, in the end our problems got the best of us." If pressed for more, you say, "Sometime in the future, if we become close enough, I might be willing to talk about it." After all, what is more pathetic than two divorced people sitting around bashing their former spouses? A man with a compulsion to bash his ex-wife is a man who hasn't faced his role in the failed marriage.

After some delightful phone conversations with one of the sexiest voices ever, I decided to meet the semi-retired lawyer I call "The Charmer." He was new to the area from Washington State and not even unpacked yet, but was anxious to meet a nice woman. We lived two hours apart and he volunteered to travel three-fourths of the distance, with me doing my part by traveling thirty minutes. We agreed to meet at an upscale restaurant and as I approached the bar I was greeted by the six-foot-four gentleman, who was scented with expensive French cologne, wearing a perfectly tailored suit and a professionally starched and pressed pin-striped shirt with French cuffs and amazing gold cuff links.

He was a man of incredible education and not afraid to open his wallet in pursuit of a good time. He was very good at making conversation, even if it was primarily about himself. I've noticed that most men who become seasoned in the state of bachelorhood love to talk about themselves.

Being a woman who had worked long hours in business for many years—along with the obligations of a thirty-year marriage and being a strong mother figure for my soon to be 30-year-old son—I didn't have much to add when the subject turned to colleges and advanced degrees. With the help of a natural gift for salesmanship, my lowly Associates

NEXT!!

Degree in business had afforded me enough knowledge to survive in the business world. In any event, this man of great stature was very proud of his education. But my question was, after retiring twelve years earlier, what did he have to offer at present besides memories?

A brilliant lawyer friend once told me—after years of counseling following his own rather disturbing and surprising divorce—that to live completely in the present is often the best cure for post-divorce trauma. In fact, he said, it's good advice for anyone. Very true.

Well, "The Charmer's" present life didn't measure up to his past, so I soon understood he wouldn't be part of my present. In fact, he had pursued a life that didn't make room for any woman, which isn't a criticism but not what I was looking for. Although I enjoy dating, going out, or sitting home enjoying warm conversation, the train has to be moving somewhere, which for me is toward a permanent relationship. When my handsome and well-tailored friend began to complain about the $2,000 annual fee to store his art collection, and how the appraisal on his condo had fallen by half and maybe he should just let the bank have it, my doubtful mind was whispering **NEXT!!** Just hours earlier, when I first laid eyes on him and took in his physical presence, I was thinking, "Could this be the one?" Now, disappointment was taking over.

Maybe it was his appearance, but despite his ego and self-absorption I decided to give him another chance. We went out two more times before I realized there was no warmth in his heart for others, including me. When he did start to ask me about myself, it seemed geared toward learning my financial situation. Were the fine suits and fine dinners just a show? They say you can't judge a book by its cover, and it was time to stow this charming book back on the shelf. **NEXT!!**

Good points: I learned a lot about the licensing required to practice law in the State of Florida. I also better understood why some professionals continue working long after they could have retired.

Angie's Lessons Learned ...
When your two worlds are "worlds apart," it's unlikely your planets will ever align.

"We'd all like a reputation for generosity, and we'd all like to buy it cheap."
~ Mignon McLaughlin, American Journalist

THE CHEAP HEART THROB

Up to this point, the word "relationship" has not played a very prominent part in my saga. But, except for "The One Who Got Away," this gentleman was the only one I truly felt love for. Our time together was good—although on and off—because he truly was "A Good Guy." He just never recovered adequately enough from his past.

I've dubbed him "The Cheap Heart Throb" and in a page or two you'll see why, but because our relationship ran a long course my feelings for him were different than with any of the others. Yes, I know that three or four months is a pretty good run for many relationships, and in that time you can ride the ups and downs of a romantic roller coaster and maybe discover enough to know if you want to go on. Or maybe not. After one month you might be positive this man is special; at two months he might be potentially "the love of my life." But with that knowledge he gets so confident that he lets his guard down and by three months you begin to see the real person. By four months it's goodbye. NEXT!!

NEXT!!

Because of his many positive attributes, our on-again, off-again relationship went on for around two and one-half years. He wasn't perfect. I tolerated his chain smoking habit—the one and only time I had done so. "Heartthrob" was a man of advanced years beyond mine, who loved his family and grandchildren. That was very apparent as he had designated times of the years, along with certain events, that he planned with him. His two ex-wives, having had children with both of them, obviously drained him financially. On our first meeting I asked how many ex-wives he had, and he replied, "I have two housekeepers," meaning they both kept the houses. Regardless, he was a good man of Italian descent and had fabulous stories to tell that would have made great movie plots. He was tall, strong and had a brilliant sports record in high school and college. His intelligence and education were outstanding. He presented himself well and treated me in a very caring way. Christmas of 2006 was a special time for us as we spent New Year's Eve together and enjoyed the first days of the New Year. I invited him to a big family wedding shortly thereafter and my family, to this day, still asks about him. They found him delightful.

So what was the problem? By now some of you might be thinking that I'm hard to please, or that I don't know how to take the bad with the good. In storybook worlds love and a good heart always prevail, but my world is reality, not storybook. So what was the problem? Distance, money issues and his determination to live in a simple, somewhat unfurnished one bedroom efficiency hours away from me. His past business partnership left him always struggling, and wandering all over the country to find work wherever he could. He lived most of the time on the road, which affected his energy level when we had time together.

Angela LaTorre

One weekend in the early spring, he invited me to come stay with him at his efficiency. I must write about this weekend with hope that I don't offend him, as his intentions were apparently different from how I responded. But in any event, in my eyes the story is too humorous not to tell. "Angie," he told me when I arrived, "this is going to be a 'no-motor' weekend."

"Okay," I said, "please define that, because that's a new one to me." As we prepared the Friday night meal, which consisted of one shared leftover chicken breast and Del Monte's best canned green beans, he proceeded to explain what he had in mind. A "no-motor weekend" is something he invented with his son as a challenge to enjoy each other's company in events that didn't require the use of any motors (i.e., cars, planes, boats, taxis, etc.). Of course that meant seventy-two hours locked down in the efficiency. Keep in mind, this location is a few miles away from the lovely beaches of Boca Raton, Florida, which had been a big part of my vision for the weekend. As I digested the chicken breast that night and got ready for bed at 8:15 p.m. I wondered what tomorrow would bring.

> He told my son, "Give the check to your mother; she's the one with the money."

The beautiful sunrise came soon enough and after coffee I got to feast my eyes on the answer. He apparently was too excited to eat and his enthusiasm was almost contagious. Almost. I watched him joyfully reviving his roller blades from years ago, replenishing the gray duct tape he used in lieu of laces. Then he introduced me to my "non-motor" conveyance: A two-wheeled "carriage" fresh from the pawn shop. There's nothing wrong with pawn shops, but I buy jewelry from pawn shops, not bicycles. Still, I'm game and we're off, him on his blades and me on worn out rubber. A

NEXT!!

Dunkin Doughnuts comes in sight and I'm hungry. Last night's chicken and green beans were long gone. *Dunkin's* 99 cent deals were happening at the time and the bagel, cheese and sausage trio with coffee was inviting. He gladly agreed but when he got inside he insisted one "deal" was enough and offered the eggs and sausage to me explaining he would enjoy the bread as I was on a "low carb" diet that day. How kind! How considerate! How cheap! I was amazed at just how frugal this man was, and despite his wonderful qualities, it was hard to ignore what had happened. Maybe I should have thanked him; I would be very thin right now if I had stayed with him.

An hour later, still skating and pedaling, we approached a dollar store. I was contemplating the joy of seeing my one-year-old grandson later that day at an early birthday celebration for my son. They lived twenty minutes away and I had planned all along to couple my weekend with the Heartthrob with my son's birthday. Of course this was before I knew of the "no motors" rule. Heartthrob directed me to spend my allocated and budgeted amount of one dollar of my own money on my grandson's present and no more. Teasing or not, I did not appreciate him telling me how much of my own money to spend. From there it was on to *Publix*, a grocery store he didn't patronize, he said, because their prices are too high. Once again he tried to grab the purse strings, cheerfully trying to make it feel like a fun challenge while instructing me on how much I should spend on my son's birthday card. This was a big no-no. In fact, a giant no-no! As the afternoon approached and our legs finally grew weary, it was time to take our human motors back to the efficiency. Saturday night and there we were again, but this time we shared a steak and each other. He was delightful in many ways and I still think about him often.

Angela LaTorre

Sunday morning. A beautiful sunrise. The *Miami Herald* arrived and it was time to clip the coupons of the day. I know this gentleman had a real love for me and commitment was part of his plan, but moment by moment the plot of the story was beginning to lose momentum. Now, I do remember the early days of marriage and the coupon organizer and, trust me, I still believe in them. But after the canned goods, the shared bagel, the dollar store, the cheap birthday card, the old rubber tires, tired legs and sharing a bathroom so small you could complete the morning hygiene ritual without moving, I was not ready for clipping coupons—or for the gleeful look in his eyes as he wielded the scissors. I was caught between tears and laughter.

Sundays are always days of joy—somehow, someway—and on this Sunday I was going to see my beautiful daughter-in-law, son and of course the grandsons I adore beyond words. So I endured the coupon clipping, and then took a long nap. Later, the sound of my car motor firing up was never so sweet, and we were soon on our way to one of my son's favorite restaurants in Boca Raton. But I must admit, the "no-motor" routine felt like a real accomplishment. No motors sounded for forty-eight hours from Friday afternoon around 3 p.m. until the same time Sunday afternoon. The only thing missing from a true old-fashioned weekend was the hand-cranked ice cream maker.

The restaurant was one of those popular, "all you can eat for one low price" buffets, and we were both hungry—going around powered by one's own motor has a way of doing that. Heartthrob was very presentable as always and when the check came, he looked at my son and said, "Give it to your mother; she's the one with the money." Interestingly enough, despite his "frugality," we still talk on occasion because he truly is a good guy. He just carried too much financial baggage and had too much of a past.

The importance of this long, on and off relationship in my search for "Mr. Right" is that it helped me start to really narrow my parameters. I decided that I must find a man that is geographically close, has a home and a job, and has at least as much as I have materially—and with any luck, a little bit more. I honestly don't think that's too much to ask. At present the "Cheap Heartthrob" is still living in the efficiency and traveling for work—when he can find work—at the ripe age of sixty-six. All the best to him, but for obvious reasons he had to be stamped a **NEXT!!**

Good points: His heart and love for his family were very real. I must also add that as I meet more and more men that have gotten divorced with children involved, it seems apparent that the legal system favors the woman in most cases. But who knows, as I said before, I never hear the ex-wife's side of the story.

Angie's Lessons Learned ...
Polls say fights about money are No. 1 for breaking up relationships. I believe it.

"When you smoke the herb, it reveals you to yourself."
  ~ Bob Marley, Jamaican Reggae Icon

THE HERBOLOGIST

If I have learned any one thing at this point, as far as dating and meeting people, it is to represent yourself for who you really are. However hard you may try to deceive, the future will reveal the truth anyway. "The Herbologist" was rather satisfied with himself and rightfully so. He had led a full and adventurous life. He served his country well during the Vietnam War and proudly showed me proof of that. He had survived the loss of two wives and was looking for a potential third one. But he seemed to be charmed with "herbs," and I am not speaking of the ones we use to season food. He managed to keep this fascination at bay for a while after we met but he was soon back at it. I went along with it, eventually to my dismay. I was new to the dating scene when I met this gentleman and tolerated a lot more than I am willing to tolerate now.

Aside from his pleasurable but illegal habit, he also enjoyed flying and was a rather good pilot. Being in the sky

NEXT!!

and being high never went hand-in-hand, thank God. However the joy of the plane, its expenses, and a sinking real estate career were all taking a toll on him. The market was at an all-time high when we met but was beginning to take a nose dive. We continued to see each other on a very casual basis and his study of herbology became more and more of a daily event. Meeting him for lunch at 11:30 AM during a business day and not being able to fully communicate with him because he was high became a problem. Because of this continuous residence in the upper atmosphere, his stories became more and more distorted.

As early fall approached he seemed to be getting his habit under control again. Who knows, maybe it had something to do with the tanking real estate market, since smoking herb on a daily basis is no cheap habit (the "Cheap Heartthrob" would have been appalled, since I don't think they put coupons for pot in the Sunday paper). So I decided to accept his invitation to take a long weekend trip with him, and travel down memory lane to visit his Connecticut roots.

> Over the long weekend he'd been unable to visit his habit, and now it was calling in a loud voice.

Dating a lot of different men really helped expand my horizons as far as understanding the various ways people see the world. When you're married as long as I was, you tend to get tunnel vision; you see things through your family's perspective or your husband's family perspective. New people bring new perspectives, but in the end what's really amazing is that experience tends to confirm what you knew all along: That we truly are a product of our childhood and upbringing.

That family connection never goes completely away. Many people remember those formative years as seeming to go on forever, when in fact they are a small portion of the average life. When we lose a parent, we lose a part of that childhood and part of the heritage that makes us who we are. In "The Herbologist's" case, that sudden loss made him more determined than ever to reaffirm and reconnect with his roots—and to share them with me.

I was rather impressed with the trail he had followed from a seemingly delightful childhood to manhood: The summer home on the Connecticut shore, the long-time friends, the neighborhood spots where he was still remembered. His athletic merit was obvious as he shared his memories of four wonderful years at the University of Connecticut. We visited the UCONN campus and I couldn't help being impressed. All and all, it was a memorable weekend and he was, as always, extremely attentive and the epitome of a gentleman.

Then we arrived back in Florida, landing at Orlando Airport on a rather foggy Friday night late in October. Over the long weekend he'd been unable to visit his habit, and now it was calling in a loud voice. He couldn't get back to the coast soon enough. Traveling home on Interstate 4 at 11:45 p.m. and flying along at 100 mph is not my idea of fun. Despite my urgent remarks about his speed and clear disapproval, he continued totally unconcerned with my desires.

The weekend in Connecticut had made me hopeful this could become a real relationship, but now I was beyond mad. If he had been forced just once to slow down for a quick red light, I would have dismissed myself from his vehicle in a flash. Needless to say, that was our last date and to this day I will not even consider dating a man that has anything to do with illegal drugs. The risk is just not worth it. Chalk up another **NEXT!!** Too bad, I was hoping for a summertime trip to the Connecticut shore.

Good points: I enjoyed many areas of this man's life, but he just loved his dope more than me. I continue to enjoy herbs of another nature, and spices too. What would you expect from a full-blooded Sicilian girl!

Angie's Lessons Learned ...
Addiction isn't about character, and good character can't save the addicted.

> *"A proud man is always looking down on things and people; and, of course, as long as you're looking down, you can't see something that's above you."*
> ~ C. S. Lewis, British Scholar and Novelist

THE HOLY ONE

As a woman of faith, having been brought up in the Catholic Church I possess a strong belief in a higher being. My ex-husband and I were very active in the church for a long period of our marriage. I truly believe if we would have been friends first and continued practicing our faith we still might be together today. With that being my history, I thought I might see if I could place myself in a Christian singles setting and meet a Godly man. I suppose you can see the pendulum swinging in the opposite direction after my experience with "The Herbologist."

Trust me, I will always believe, hope, and pray that God will send me a God-fearing man, just not the one who came my way this time. He was tall, rather dark and handsome in what seemed a meaningful way. His problems, however, and his strong sense of being a nonconformist led him on a trail of great losses. He proclaimed that paying taxes to the

NEXT!!

IRS was totally voluntary, and he refused to do so for years. Those years eventually cost his wonderful medical practice, his lovely home and finally the departure of his wife after more than a few major legal battles that left him practically homeless and totally broke. Interestingly enough, he claimed all of his motives were inspired by God. Despite the fact that my Bible says to honor our authorities and respect the law of the land, he apparently had his own translation, and his own laws. Needless to say, this one did not make it to date number three. By the time the IRS was done with him he was down to a mere $700 a month in income. He said they couldn't take his pride. He still had plenty of that—too much as far as I was concerned—and not enough of anything else. **NEXT!!**

    Good points: I received an advanced lesson on religious posing and hypocrisy.

Angie's Lessons Learned ...
Sometimes you can make your own rules; sometimes you can't.

"Dancing is like dreaming with your feet!"
~ Constanze, singer and Wolfgang Mozart's wife

THE DANCER

As a little girl I loved the constant presence of music that filled the rooms of our three-story home in New Jersey. My father had his version of singing opera, as he defined it. My uncle was known to have graced the stage at the Metropolitan Opera House in New York City, and my aunt had quite the voice as well. The Italian culture, at least in my family, was one of great music, and on many occasions, of dancing too—wherever and whenever. With many first cousins living within a few miles and a basement all to ourselves, we would gather and dance the night away in our own crazy way. I often wondered how grand it would have been to have studied dance at a young age, but there were other priorities. I love to watch the magic of dance and try to attend all the recitals that my poised, eight-year-old niece has become a part of. Her performance in "The Nutcracker" amazed me during the Christmas season of 2008.

So now it was my turn to experience dance—free, single and with a passion that had been building for years. During my many dating experiences I discovered that dancing is

NEXT!!

the most fun you can have with the opposite sex while keeping your clothes on, and it has a way of keeping you from rushing too quickly to the bedroom. Dance is an expression, an illusion, a movement of your heart, soul and deepest personality. Dance is an expression of who we truly are—sometimes kept to ourselves and other times springing up like the rising sun during different seasons of our life.

Dance can exhibit many faces and create a breathless atmosphere of truth, healing, and therapy within a future promise of mindless fun. Dance allows my body to think and my mind to rest, to rest in the power of the movement, the caress of a man and, all to often, the need to submit. Without dance, I would have to find another way to fill a void, a hunger, a need for a true statement of my being. I'm not sure any other way is possible.

> ... when you combine talent with a great personality ... you end up with a man who has certain expectations about women.

After several months of typical ballroom instruction and truly enjoying it, I was introduced to *The West Coast Swing*, a dance that originated on the West Coast and in my opinion is a form of free style dancing under the lead of a partner which incorporates a lot of free play and fun on the woman's part. *West Coast Swing* is an exciting tribute to free expression that incorporates many aspects of other dances with a total focus on the music, instead of mere steps and required movements of ballroom protocols. In another words, it's pure bliss and fun in a great casual atmosphere.

As I became more and more intrigued, I was blessed to meet a gentleman who helped pioneer this dance in Central Florida. Our small town dance community welcomed his arrival, his instructions, and inspiring attitude. He was a great teacher, which helped us to understand the meaning of his collection of movements. More importantly, his focus was on having a great time with zero tolerance for arrogance, which so often finds a home in the typical ballroom. His network allowed us to enjoy our time dancing in different venues with a constant rule being to "dance with someone new."

As he and I became friends we also had occasion to enjoy each other's company, and I was happy to have him escort me to several special events. As a single woman, it's a joy to have a professional dance instructor on your arm as you enter a holiday ball and approach the dance floor. It's pure joy, even though the intimidation can be overwhelming at times. I enjoyed our friendship more and more as time went on, and having him as a dance partner carried me to a higher plane as a dancer, which at that time was my main focus in life—along with finding a man to date and perhaps marry.

But those two goals didn't fit together well. "The Dancer" was a bit of a challenge as far as dating. Why? Well for starters when you combine talent with a great personality and a rather inviting physical presence, a cute smile and moves that can make an 85-year-old feel like a teenage girl, you end up with a man who has certain expectations about women. Along with that comes a schedule that requires a lot of time away on weekends, and very late nights.

Believe me, I don't hold a grudge. T*he West Coast Swing* would not be the same for me if it wasn't for this great guy, and I encourage all of you to at least take a look at *www.floorplayswingclub.com*. I will always hold strong and friendly feelings for this gentleman. The benefits were endless, and with his dance moves, he has added to my life in many ways. We may never date again, but he will *never* be called a **NEXT!!**

NEXT!!

Good points: He reminded me to stop pressing so hard in my search for "Mr. Right" and just enjoy myself along the way. Just like swing dancing came my way when I was ready for it, the same would happen with the man meant for me. All things in their own time. As you'll see later, I think he may have been right.

Angie's Lessons Learned ...
Find your passion, and the rest of your desires will follow as day follows night.

"If dogs could talk, perhaps we would find it as hard to get along with them as we do with people."
~ Karel Čapek, Czech writer

MAN AND HIS DOGS

Oh, the amazing wonders of a man and his dogs! Now don't get me wrong, I love animals and I truly miss my black lab that has now been gone over a year. After my divorce, she became my closest companion and after her death I was truly alone for the first time in my life.

So with that said, here's the story of the one I now call "Dog Man." He was tall, dark, handsome and very educated. He was a good cook, had a stable job as an educator and a rather nice home. He clearly seemed to love his parents and had many other good qualities. He had never fathered children but he embraced his Golden Retrievers with the kind of reverence most people reserve for their offspring. That's Golden Retrievers, plural. He made it very clear early on that his two dogs are a big part of his life; they always had been and always would be.

Our second date was an invitation to his home for a nice

NEXT!!

dinner and I had the pleasure of meeting both the dogs in a special way. They were large, to the tune of about ninety pounds each, and one was a very aggressive pup. They joined us on the couch and their presence could not be ignored. All in all, they were fairly well behaved—with the exception of a few scratches from the misbehaving pup.

Date number three: It's early November and I needed a date for a rather special and somewhat formal wedding. As I believe I expressed earlier, two situations that cause me to feel very lonely and sometimes emotional are attending weddings alone and traveling by myself. Not fun in my book. So I asked the "Dog Man" to be my guest at the wedding. Of course, he was delighted and we planned accordingly. He lived about an hour and a half away so I invited him for dinner on Saturday night. The wedding was Sunday afternoon. I provided what I thought were easy directions to my home via e-mail and asked what he would like for dinner. Since he knew I had a full day at work, the proper answer was, "something simple," or even, "would you like me to stop and pick up something?" Instead he asked me to choose one of my favorite specialty dishes. I thought that was a little assuming, so early on, but the giver in me complied. After working all day Saturday and coming home to cook and prepare in a "Martha Stewart" fashion, my date calls. He is very lost and very late. Here I go again, traveling down the "broad brush highway," but my experience with educators is that they have distaste for following instructions. Maybe it's because they are so versed in constantly giving instructions. In any event, the chicken was drying out while staying warm, and ninety min-

> I said a nice goodbye to "Dog Man" and his dogs, reserving for later the explanation I intended to give him.

utes later, "Dog Man" finally arrives, preceded by the malodorous presence of his two massive dogs—both clearly needing to be bathed. Much to my amazement, I realized I had failed to discuss this situation. What was I to do, tell the three of them to turn around and go home? I was desperately trying to convince myself that this could work. I really didn't want to go alone to that wedding. But the fact is, I lived in a "townhome community," and had a roommate who was just as protective of her space as she was respectful of mine.

It was the first weekend in November and we were experiencing unseasonably cool weather. Maybe "Dog Man" sensed my dismay, because he began explaining that we might have met at the wrong time of the year because when it's below fifty degrees his pups must stay inside because it just too chilly for them. He made that requirement clear, with no apologies. Let me assure you, things were getting pretty chilly as far as I was concerned. Oh, here's the best part: Having presented himself in a very untimely manner, without so much as a feigned "I'm sorry," he greets me and hands me an old wrinkled *Walmart* bag. For a second I was hopeful. "Ah," I thought, surely he has reciprocated my hospitality in a polite manner and brought a gift for the host, yours truly, for whom he claimed he fell the moment we met. Wrong! As I began to research the contents of the plastic bag, I discovered a lovely collection of *Alpo's* finest dog food, along with two of the biggest and greasiest pig knuckles I'd ever seen. Something for the dogs to enjoy while we went to the wedding, he explained, as if he was kindly assuring me he had no plans to invite the dogs to tag along to the nuptials. At the very bottom of the bag was a slime covered rag that clearly had been used to wipe their jaws, at least that's what I hoped. No way was I going to touch it and

NEXT!!

find out! My, oh my. Was there nothing here for the woman of his dreams? Where was the wine or a Yankee Candle? At this point a dead rose would have been fine. Any question where I ranked?

Dinner was served, the scraps were devoured and the morning brought even cooler temperatures and a mandatory doggy walk. Any potential romance was overpowered by the presence of these children of his. I had become convinced at a previous juncture of this second-time-around dating journey that animals would be easier to deal with than minor children. I was now rethinking that conviction.

Sunday was full of delightful anticipation. The 3 p.m. wedding ceremony would be followed by a stimulating cocktail hour and then an elegant sit down dinner with some of my best friends. In my romantic imagination, it would all culminate in a wondrous opportunity to display my remarkable dancing, the pride and passion of my life. I had been looking forward to this day for many months.

As I prepared, I frequently announced the time by which we needed to leave. I am very respectful of time regarding weddings and funerals, and I think others should be too—even if you are just a guest. Well, "Dog Man" enjoyed lounging—no problem under normal circumstances, but in this case I could see he would make us late. And his dogs were all over my couch. The throw was balled up by the arm rest and dog aroma was now traveling throughout my home.

When "Dog Man" finally did get dressed, he looked good. I sprayed on some of my son's cologne to make sure he didn't arrive wearing the scent of *Golden Retriever #5*. We are now running late but he still had to prepare for our absence. The greasy knuckles were placed, the boys got their last minute love pats and "Dog Man" and I were at last off to the wedding. Of course, I drove because I wanted to enjoy the *Dior* fragrance I was wearing and had no desire to travel in his smelly SUV for the hour-long trip.

The wedding was lovely and he was a perfect gentleman. But we had to leave early, sacrificing some of my dance time due to his long drive home. Dating someone who lives more than an hour away ends up being a challenge for me. I kept learning that lesson over and over, each time making allowances for someone with other attractive attributes. But at this point I truly believe long distance relationships are a recipe for heartache. He packed up the dogs while I apologized to the neighbors who had stepped outside to complain about the endless barking over the last four hours.

I said a nice goodbye to "Dog Man" and his dogs, reserving for later the explanation I intended to give him. I didn't wish to offend him, since these dogs clearly were a big part of his life, which is fine, but they could not be a big part of my life for reasons I don't think I need to explain any further. Since then, I now question new prospects regarding their pets. I'm not exactly like the apartment manager who runs an ad saying, "Cats OK, dogs up to forty pounds," but can you imagine sharing a bed with a big guy and two huge dogs all at the same time? Thanks but no thanks.

Monday morning I sent "Dog Man" a nice e-mail and he became my latest **NEXT!!**

Good points: Amazingly enough, the possibility of a date's ten-year-old daughter screaming in the mall because dad won't let her pierce her ears, now seems like a pleasant prospect.

Angie's Lessons Learned ...

Jesus wasn't speaking about dogs, but it's still true: "No man can serve two masters."

> "Inflation is when you pay fifteen dollars for the ten-dollar haircut you used to get for five dollars when you had hair."
> ~ Sam Ewing, American writer

MAN AND HIS HAIR

At the time of this adventure I had been dancing for over three years. The dance world involves many venues and specific dance types. A common hot spot is "Singles Dances." These dances—at least in Central Florida—seem to attract men and women that are a bit seasoned (yes, I mean older!). I love the word "seasoned" and use it frequently when addressing skin care issues with my clients. "Old" and "mature" are forbidden words in my business. When you tell someone they are well seasoned, like a bottle of finely aged wine, it sounds so much better.

As we all know, as the aging process goes so does the hair for many—for men especially, of course. I remember one special Valentine's Dance at the local Moose Lodge. Everyone was donning their red and white and looking rather grand. I took a quick glance around the room at all the sea-

NEXT!!

soned men and thought to myself, there are enough toupees here to carpet one of my bedrooms. It's amazing how pitiful some of these pieces can look, especially where the fake parts meet the last remnants of real hair. I was always careful on the dance floors not to swing some of these seasoned gentlemen too hard because, being the visual person I am, I could just picture one of these furry pieces flying through the air and landing on a woman's breasts!

One Saturday night my roommate and I decided to visit a popular dance spot where all the "good ole boys" hang out, in a small city called Sanford, forty miles inland from Daytona Beach. Well it was the night of the yearly "Tractor Pull," and the rednecks—male and female—were in their glory. This was our first visit to "The Barn," and at first we were thinking it was probably our last. But some friends from our dance group joined us and we began having a great time. As we took in the sights and watched people become more and more intoxicated, we slowly enjoyed our first drink of the night, which was purchased for us by two rather nice looking men. This also was their first experience at "The Barn," and in time they came over and we started to chat. My roommate was very happy in her current relationship, but of course I was looking. These two were obviously successful business men just visiting from the Jacksonville area but still "good ole boys" if you know what I mean. To come across as a "good ole boy" is practically a requirement for the Southern male, no matter how high he has climbed on the cultural ladder, and the farther north you travel in Florida the closer you come to the real South.

Florida is such a Mecca of people and, depending on the area, the men come across quite differently. For example, in Northern Florida locales like Gainesville or Jacksonville the men seem a little more country—into fishing and hunting—

and just being "down home" kind of guys. In Central Florida—the Orlando area—you find the more business oriented types. Stability is their common trait. My area, Central Florida's East Coast, is different. You have the golfers, surfers, beach guys. Everyone is casual and free spirited. South Florida primarily is an international market of men. I spend a lot of time there visiting my son. On any Saturday evening at one of the finest ballrooms in the United States, I can dance with men of every nationality.

In any event, the gentleman being so attentive to me at the Sanford "Barn" seemed to have a good bit to offer and I was instantly attracted to him—which does not happen that often, even though it may seem to the reader that instant attraction is what this book is all about.

> When I called him on it, he boldly said, "Yes, I am after a one night stand ..."

I agreed to give him my phone number and we talked every night the following week. He was very clear as to what he was looking for and was very convincing regarding his desire for a long-term, committed relationship.

The chemistry between us was really bubbling, and as the phone conversations became more and more interesting, I agreed to meet him for our first date. I was so eager to get to know him better that I broke one of my basic rules, which states let the man come to you on the first date. No meeting halfway. It was just before Christmas and I wanted to see the Christmas lights that are part of the year-round delight and charm of beautiful St. Augustine. So we met, had dinner and he was very attentive, a little too attentive in a hands-on way, if you know what I mean. Face-to-face is so important early on in a potential relationship and truly will confirm or disprove your initial impression. Up to now, on-

NEXT!!

line and on the phone, this man was truly convincing. He had the whole sales pitch down pat as far as pursuing one special woman. Much to my surprise, the one-on-one experience led me to a contrary conclusion. I remain amazed how people can be so different online or even on the phone, even though the phone allows for some real human communication. Misrepresenting yourself has become an art for many and it was clear by the end of the evening that this man was after nothing more than a one night stand. When I called him on it, he boldly said, "Yes, I am after a one night stand—one after another and another and another," and never once suggested they might all be with one woman. Quite the contrary. What woman wouldn't want to feel that each new night with her man was like the first time? But this guy was out to put as many notches on his belt as possible, to have his dance card punched until there was no card left—you get the picture. He was just a monkey who wanted all the bananas, no apology.

    The great final moment came as we were saying goodbye. He was honest enough to admit the rather nice looking rug on his head was not his own, as if he took some strange pleasure from revealing how much he'd fooled me. Actually, I think, since I was dumping him and he knew I was in the beauty business, he wanted to publicize his list of entrepreneurial successes, which included the manufacture of fine head rugs. I was indeed impressed by how natural it looked, how it was customized to his head and made from human hair. What further amazed me was just how incredibly different he looked when he decided to remove it. He worked oh so gently, with a running description of the removal and replacement processes, including proper glue and exact handling for strategically placing it back on his head. I thought to myself, it's a good thing we have no future because if I had ever decided to grab onto his head during a wantonly fun encounter, it might have caused somewhat of a shock. Having the fine rug in place did wonders for this man's appearance. That's about the only good thing I can say about him. The rest of his behavior left me totally unimpressed. He was quite the player, all hat and no cowboy, and very much suited to be stamped **NEXT!!**

Good points: I managed to retain the name of the toupee company in Germany that has mastered this much needed service and will gladly recommend it to some of those seasoned gentlemen I meet on the dance floor or in the salon.

Angie's Lessons Learned ...
Encourage a man to show his true colors quickly. Less time wasted playing games.

"Every mother hopes that her daughter will marry a better man than she did, and is convinced that her son will never find a wife as good as his father did."

~ Martin Anderson-Nexo, Danish writer

MOMMA'S BOY

Loving one's mother is a consistently good sign of a good man, but there has to be a limit. Taking care of her and spending time with her are to be admired. Having to live with Momma unless she's ill is another story. Despite some other nice traits, this gentleman was really just too much of a momma's boy.

Like many of my dates, we met via the internet and then had a nice chat on the phone. He was of Greek heritage and clearly understood the whole family and cultural aspects of the Italian culture as there are similarities between the two. Greek men are just very close to their mothers, almost to a fault, but at first I valued his loyalty to her as a sign of his sensitivity. Eventually my opinion would change.

Our first in-person meeting was very nice and we were both interested in the health/wellness field with both clearly dedicated to building our practices. He appeared to be

NEXT!!

totally together, dark, poised and remarkably handsome. Modeling had preceded his medical career.

We shared an interest in dancing and he agreed to join me for the inaugural, "So You Think You Can Dance Daytona" contest. If you haven't noticed, dance competition is becoming a growing trend in this country, thanks to "Dancing with the Stars" and various other movies, commercials, etc. In the spring of 2009 a new movie was released featuring the *West Coast Swing* and the dance world that surrounds it. I mention it only to show the kind of excitement generated by the world of dance, which I was certainly feeling big time as we prepared to "dance Daytona."

> I love my own mother dearly, and she wants the best for me, but she gives me space and realizes that a companion is a big part of my future ...

So our evening was planned and the dress code discussed. We'd start with cocktails, dinner, and then the performance. A few of his colleagues in the area also would be competing. I would meet him there because I was picking up the tickets, since I had invited him. I had no problem with that; I believe in being a partner. Who wrote the rule that the man should pay for everything? My manicure, pedicure and stunning outfit were all in place, and I was on my way. Then my cell phone rings and my date informs me that his mother is not feeling well. He's not sure that he will be able to make the date as he must check on her and will call me in about a hour to give me an update after he sees her. We had about two hours before curtain time.

Disappointing? Wouldn't anyone be disappointed? Here I am again stuck in a familiar place: smelling great, looking great, and left all by my little lonesome self. The food was terrific, and I soon found some of my fellow dancers to join and chat with. Dancing is such a good social hobby for single people for so many reasons and the camaraderie is right near the top.

More than an hour had passed since I last heard from "Momma's Boy" and still no call. At that point I would have been fine with, "thanks but no thanks, Momma needs me at her side." Just call and tell me something! I cannot stand a man that is not honest and takes the cowardly approach. Needless to say, my evening was a bit of a disappointment, but I enjoyed the show, hung out with some of my "buds" and enjoyed the humor of our dance community as we watched some of our finest making fools of themselves. I consoled myself with knowing it was for a good cause and that it might pay off with a boost to dance interest in Daytona. The more the merrier, and some of them would have to be single men. Real men that is, not momma's boys. One can always hope.

It's Monday evening and the phone rings. Of course it's my long lost date from Saturday night and after much detail the conclusion is Momma seems to be doing fine. The story is that she is contemplating knee surgery and her heart was a little off rhythm Saturday night. At least that's what she told him—my observation, not his. In an effort to show he's sorry, he invited me to dinner and shared that his mother and fifteen-year-old daughter would be joining us. I was somewhat delighted because I feel everyone deserves a second chance and I had no reason not to believe him. OK, I know I was being too easy but I was raised to believe family always comes first, although at that point I was still thinking his failure to call Saturday night was inexcusable. Once I met Momma, I was sure. While presenting her with a get-well basket, I was thinking that she looks healthier than me.

NEXT!!

There before me was a woman of Mediterranean descent, blessed with good genes and sporting a healthy glow. She had "dressed" for the occasion, dangling earrings and all. It crossed my mind that it was more likely she'll attend my funeral than that I'll attend hers!

The three-hour dinner, which I learned happened two to three times a week at Momma's house, was full of questions. The question for him in my mind was how do you manage to grow a full-time medical supplements business (he told me they were "going global"), devote time to your fifteen-year-old—who lives out of town, visit Momma several times a week while being on call the rest of the time, and still find time to nurture a long-term love relationship with a woman?

Fortunately, the too obvious answer was also running through my mind: Not going to happen! And it didn't, not for us. Until he cuts that umbilical cord, I can't see it happening at all. What woman would tolerate all of Momma's questions the first night they met? It was one query after another: How old are you? How long were you married? Who divorced whom and why? How long did the divorce take? How long did it take you to grow your hair? On and on. Although I liked some things about her, and I do think he and I would have had some potential, there was just too much Momma for me.

I love my own mother dearly and she wants the best for me, but she gives me space and realizes that a companion is a big part of my future—and really puts no demands on my time.

I truly wish this man the best, and I've noticed he's still searching the internet. He's smart, handsome and very charming, but just too much a momma's boy. A woman wants to be number one in her man's life and his Momma is desperately holding on to that position. A good friend, yes, if that's what he wants, but I have to say, **NEXT!!**

Good points: Once again experience helped me understand the nuances of what I was looking for. I had thought a guy with a strong sense of family was what I wanted. Now I understand the limitations of that desire.

Angie's Lessons Learned ...

I really wish that Momma would have learned a lesson, but I know she never will.

> "People go to casinos for the same reason they go on blind dates—hoping to hit the jackpot. But mostly, you just wind up broke or alone at the bar."
> ~ Carrie Bradshaw (actress Sarah Jessica Parker, *Sex and the City*)

BLIND DATE HORRORS

Every day I thank God for my friends and my incredible family. Being one of four girls and of course the only single one, the three sisters are always trying to set me up. Having been down that road more than once, I decided once again to trust a long-time friend who seemed to really know me. Among all her accomplishments and responsibilities, she has functioned successfully as a kind of matchmaker, which has resulted in several happy marriages. So why not me? A very seasoned widow neighbor of hers, whose health was failing, had always embraced the thought of seeing her son married before her death. At the age of fifty-seven, he had escaped marriage (first red flag) and apparently any long-term commitments. His mommy continuously insisted that he was handsome, educated and highly

NEXT!!

accomplished. He'd worked in the computer field for years as a programmer skilled in technology support strategies.

Of course, my friend is taking notes on all this and her mental wheels are turning. She knows the exceptional financial situation that will be the legacy of this lonely bachelor. Now, money isn't everything but it sure has a way of making life easier at times. While my friend is describing this situation—as if the bachelor was a promising investment opportunity—a second red flag popped up: She has never met the gentleman. She only knows mom. But she brushed this aside because she has known mommy "many years" and trusts her completely. But then, all of us Italian girls truly believe in our hearts that our sons are gods and can't imagine any woman would not agree with us.

Two days later the plans are being made for what would turn out to be a rainy Friday night. I was instructed to drive to Orlando to meet this gentleman. He has been given the understanding that I'm to be there on business for the day. Of course, I have never laid eyes on him and he is too shy to call first to talk before our meeting (two more red flags). Trusting friend that I am, I decided "why not," this is going to be my "first blind date." As the sun was setting, a sky full of clouds let loose with a downpour like no other. I approached the restaurant with apprehensions rising. I thought to myself, this is crazy, how will I even find this mystery man? On that note I called my friend and said, "Please, if momma is so insistent that I meet her son, please call her now and acknowledge my presence in the parking lot by calling me to let me know how to find him." My cell phone rang within minutes and with much trembling in his voice and a real sense of shyness he says, "I am wearing a plaid flannel shirt (it's July in Florida!) and I will be waving and seated near the hostess stand." Here goes; I hold my breath

Angela LaTorre

and dash through the raindrops for the door. The man did not lie. I was greeted by quite the old-fashioned plaid shirt, and very worn at that. It reminded me of the shirts my former husband wore back in the late 70's and appeared to be that old. Who knows, maybe it was one of those actual shirts. My ex-husband did have a recent rummage sale and this man's mom lived in the area ... very curious. Oh well. The waving led me to his table where he had been coloring while waiting for my arrival. After our initial hellos and "nice to meet you" exchange, I could not help almost losing it right there as I experienced something very new to me: A true "techie" zombie with the pale skin and haphazard dress to match. This gentleman had obviously been living in "software land" since the computer age started, or possibly before. Now he was up from the catacombs, no doubt at his mother's insistence, with an appearance so rare and unplanned it would satisfy any statistician's requirements for complete random selection. Doing his best to make conversation, he explained that his first and last blind date was during his college years many years ago. He married her and it lasted less than a year. He had not dated since. Lucky me, I am date number two in the last 35 years, which I guess should have made me feel special. As he is speaking, I'm taking in the weathered flannel shirt, white plastic *Hushpuppies*, double-knit forest green polyester pants, and a rather accentuated one-sided double chin. He proceeds to tell me we are in an Italian restaurant and I can order pasta. I tried my best to keep a straight face, all the while thinking about my friend and what I was planning for her as revenge.

> I tried my best to keep a straight face, all the while thinking about my friend and what I was planning for her as revenge.

NEXT!!

Could I hire a *real* zombie to send her way? Maybe my date could give me a referral. Or maybe I could hire an actor. I'm thinking I'll have one stroll—or whatever you call the way zombies walk—into her office with his eyes rolled back so you can see only the whites, maybe drooling on himself and wearing a worn flannel shirt, and introduce himself as her client's son. Lunch anyone?

As the conversation continued, so did the coloring, his eyes fixed on *Donald Duck*. This man obviously lacked so much in the realm of social skills, and clearly he didn't want to be here anymore than me. It was remarkable in a hysterical way. I kept my composure and ordered an appetizer as a short visit was imminent. His exhausted looking face and missing teeth—the two lower ones stood in an isolated and very evident salute to the right when he spoke—made it very obvious his work didn't call for much public appearance. The added charm was the right-sided, very pronounced hanging chin. The top button of his flannel shirt was gaining space on the right side of the hanging chin, and when he spoke the tip of his collar would dance up and down. I promise you, if this blind date wasn't from zombie land, he was from outer space. It was so bad it was funny. I really didn't blame him and tried to be kind because I understood he wouldn't have come out in the light of day if not for my friend and his mother forcing this situation, but I felt like I was sitting with someone from a another world, a world all his own. The last accessory in his appearance was—you guessed it—the need for seriously thick, Coke bottle glasses. The frames looked to have lasted from his college days 40 years earlier, the ear stems connected by safety pins with a dirty bandage holding them together at the nosepiece. You honestly couldn't stage this stuff, but I started wondering if he had put on a costume to teach his mother to stay out of his life. When he spoke everything moved in asymmetrically. If he was acting, it was Oscar time.

With a polite rest room exit, I then phoned my friend and after much hilarious apology, she promised to somehow make it up to me. Thank God the appetizers arrived. The young waiter was standing by, taking this all in and I explained as I walked past him that this was my first and probably last blind date. He laughed and said, "The spring rolls are great here."

When I returned, our simple conversation continued regarding the relationship between my friend and his mother and how his mother was delighted that we—or should I say they—decided we needed to meet, etc. He basically said, I don't date and wouldn't have come except for my mother's interference. Dating means buying clothes and of course spending money. He said again that his last date was in college, which I suppose should make all the women of Central Florida feel lucky, myself excluded. His world, he explained, revolves around IBM as far as his work, and when he's not working, he enjoys time alone on his computer. His last sentence before I made my graceful exit was, "I can communicate with people all over the world, chatting via the networks, so I don't feel the need to date. I am here because Momma wants to get me married." Well, at least he said it. And Momma, here's my advice to you: **Mind your own business!!**

Anyway, the rain subsided as I journeyed home. My sense of humor has always saved me and on this night my laughter kept coming back. You could pay $50 a ticket and not experience a comedy like that. I poured a stiff drink and when it was time for another I decided to draw a warm bath, sip some Pinot Grigio and reflect, reminisce and re-

NEXT!!

member better moments. Surely I had just reached the bottom of the dating barrel. Better things had to be ahead. **NEXT!!**

Three weeks passed and on a beautiful Spring Sunday morning while I was at the gym, my sweet mother calls. She has been at her usual routine, reading the Sunday paper cover to cover. She too, is another great story of unusual accomplishments. Married at a young age, she came to America as a new bride, not knowing much and of course not a word of English. Forty years later, she would say her greatest achievement was giving five happy children the experience of a great childhood and lives filled with tremendous love. My father died in 1996 and my mom was a young widow of fifty-nine. After years of building a career, resulting in a position of Assistant Vice President of a prominent bank, everyone would agree she had led a full life. Seven years ago she met a fine gentleman and they are enjoying some wonderful years together. Understanding her life leads to accepting her passion for finding a wonderful mate for her only single child.

So there I am at the gym. I answer her call and she says with much delight, "Angela, I have found the man of your dreams." She is reading a personal ad from him, for which he has invested boldly to place it in the daily newspaper. As you might expect, the ad reads: "Great man, never late, accomplished, good looking, educated, free to spend time. Loves travel, walks on the beach, moonlight, etc. etc. etc. Without my permission she has proceeded to call him and give him my number! Sound presumptuous? Not to her. She was so sure he could be the one. Well, of course I am surprised but as always appreciative, because, trust me, the love my mother has for me is more than exceptional; she always has my best interests in mind. But despite her experience in the business world, she is very naive about the single dating world. After my dad died, she did not date for two years before meeting my current step-father.

So, within the hour I received a call from Mr. Personal Ad. I must grant him the compliment of having written a good ad. The conversation is rather nice and of course on my way home I pick up the newspaper as he was smart enough to include a photo. I'm quite familiar with—and suspicious of—the dated photo trick. How old? How touched up? Hate to sound cynical, but ... After a few more pleasant conversations with him, I convinced myself to take a chance and meet him. Why not? I suppose my last blind date might answer the question, "Why not," but if it wasn't for the confidence to barge ahead with a hearty, "Why not," I would not be writing this book!

This time, however, it was going to be on my terms. I would choose the location and time. I decided against potentially ruining an entire Saturday night and planned to meet him after an early evening wedding. Weddings are very difficult for me after a divorce, especially listening to the vows when your own vows were not forever. Seven o'clock arrives and he's there anxiously waiting. His first impression of me is positive but not surprising since I would consider myself to be fairly attractive, which helps. He, on the other hand, is sitting on a bar stool and appears to be rather short. I think back to the personal ad—no mention of height—and right away I'm afraid of seeing him stand up. As I've said before, no disrespect to shorter men because relationship truly needs to be about the person, but I just want a guy to be taller than me, which isn't hard at five-foot-six. He instantly moved in close as he spoke to me—way too close for comfort in my opinion, and all the gold hanging from his neck, fingers and wrists would have come in handy

NEXT!!

to reflect the moonlight if a black-out happened to occur. Just another of my biases, but I don't like to see a man wearing more jewelry than me. He had been drinking and the conversation was limited as he continued to repeat himself over and over again to the point of total annoyance. He was well on his way to total intoxication and I was on my way out the door. This particular date holds the record for shortest, lasting only nineteen minutes. A most definite **NEXT!!** I asked him to lose my number and I was done with blind dates and personal ads.

I say thanks for the good intentions of family and friends, but no thanks unless you have met them and know them personally.

Good points: For the life of me, I can't think of one.

Angie's Lessons Learned ...
It's easier to engage in wishful thinking when you're wishing for someone else.

"The one good thing about repeating your mistakes is you know when to cringe."

~ Anonymous

MORE INTERNET MADNESS

After the agony of my catastrophic blind dates, can you blame me for taking another chance on internet dating? The blind date fiascoes were fresh in my mind and some of my worst online memories were fading. But it would not take long to refresh my memory.

If we were a bunch of girls sitting in my living room discussing our internet adventures, I'd start by telling this story about the guy who sent an initial message regarding how he likes to travel and travels often. When I asked for details, his second e-mail message went something like this:

"Well darlin', in answer to your question, yes of course I love to travel and I travel often, so often that at times it's more than once a week." Really, I say to myself as I continue to read further. "Yes, you know I am a diesel maestro." That's fine, I say to myself. I'm not a snob about the color of a man's collar. Truck drivers make very good money and are

NEXT!!

in demand. Right away I'm romantically imagining long trips through beautiful mountain vistas, the two of us singing *Me and Bobby McGee* in perfect harmony. But as I read further I learn that his only form of "travel" involves responding to service calls via I-95, primarily over seventy-five miles of flatlands south of Jacksonville—not at all a scenic area of Florida.

"Yes, darlin'! I would love for you to be ready to hop up into my rig and hang with me as I make these calls and you can enjoy the sights of North Florida along I- 95. I promise to bring plenty of hand cleaner. And when I come to get you for a date, when we are not on the road, I promise there will be no grease under my fingernails."

I had to laugh. You have to give the guy credit for confidence. If he was a car salesman, he could point to a *Yugo* and call it a *Lexus* while keeping a straight face. I liked that, but not enough to don my overalls, strap on my version of a tool belt and hop right on board. He promised "no pajamas necessary," and when he's ready, I better be pretty damn close to ready 'cause you just don't know when the next call will be coming in. I reckon we would have had a blast. **NEXT!!!!!!!!!!!!!!!!!!!!!!!!!**

Since my divorce, I've talked to enough single people, mostly divorced women like myself, to know I'm not the only one who keeps hoping the internet will yield good results despite so often doing just the opposite. Just when I'm about to give up someone will say, "Did you hear that Becky is getting married? Wonderful guy. She met him on *Match.com*."

It was a Sunday, September 27th to be exact. My trip to North Carolina over a long weekend was cancelled due to weather and issues with my car. The prior weekend was quiet as well. You know, one can spend only so much time alone no matter how much you like yourself. So there I was, halfway through a four-day weekend with no significant plans and all my friends gone or busy. Next thing you know, there I am again checking out possible new men online. What's a girl to do when seventy percent of her business world is female-oriented, and her second job involves being engaged in front of a computer? Going to bars alone is not my style, and I had exhausted the dance community in this little town of newlyweds and "nearly deads."

Walk a mile in my shoes and then criticize. I know some of my sisters who have been there are nodding and saying, "Tell 'em Angie."

This time it's *plentyoffish.com* that's calling. I stumble across the best profile I have ever read, from what seems to be a nice man in his sixties. We write back and forth and I learn he's about sixty minutes north of me along the coast, and that we were both planning to fill the empty day by going to the beach. Lunch time is approaching and after a nice conversation, we agree to meet. Throughout this book you've seen I'm better at making rules than keeping them. One rule clearly states the man must come to me the first time, but it was a beautiful autumn day in late September—a perfect day for a top down ride in my convertible. As I headed off to meet him, I was filled with visions of the beautiful Atlantic and the warm mist of salt air gently kissing my skin.

We spoke on the phone as we both traveled toward our rendezvous point. He mentioned he was a man of "substance," just what kind and how much he failed to detail. He said, "Don't worry, you can't miss me; I will be wearing a shirt with large parrots on it and will flag you down while standing on the top of the bridge over the Intracoastal Waterway." Wow I thought, I have never been flagged down by

NEXT!!

a potential suitor. Well, there he was and most certainly not to be missed. Since I'm always fighting fifteen pounds I wish I didn't have, I don't like to call names. Euphemisms are OK with me. I don't mind a man who is "sturdy," that's one thing, but a belly out to Kansas is another. I sat parked at the foot of the bridge watching his rather slow approach. My eyes bounced from his North end to his South as he waddled up with his corpulent body swinging left, right, left. The parrots were stretched over his enormous belly, with what was meant to be a pair of birds separated by the mound of flesh exposed by a series of missing buttons.

Of course, thoughts began to run through my mind, like this one is going to be so bad it's going to be good enough to write about—which just goes to show we all have a purpose in life. I mean, if it wasn't for bad cooks would we know how to recognize a good one? It goes the same way with men—and women too I suppose although that's not really my problem.

> From that point on I was taking a lesson in what **not** to do if I am ever reborn as a man in another life.

The closer he got to me the more I zoomed in on his teeth and noticed his two central teeth had been worn in the form of an inverted "V", inspiring me to picture him nibbling on a carrot. I was about to ask, "What's up Doc," when I was distracted by noticing the black spot on the left side of his front tooth. And so he arrived, belly first, and greeted me with a big smile proudly displaying the wonder of him.

"Howdy, how are you?" he said.

I slowly replied, "I've been better."

"Well," he said, "do you want to swim first or have lunch?"

I know that my descriptions of these men often sound harsh and judgmental. I'm sorry about that. I'm just trying to tell the truth. But in my defense I will say that as long as a man was polite and not bossy and abusive, I stuck it out. That was the case that day. I was extremely disappointed and felt betrayed by the way he had portrayed himself online, but I didn't insult him. Besides that, I was hungry, but not for him. So I said, "Sure, let's eat." Fresh seafood always sounds good to me.

As I waited for him to meet me in his car, I began to wonder about the 1985 diesel Mercedes Benz he described over the phone. I have no problems with older cars, as a matter of fact, I happen to like older cars if they are well maintained. Then I looked in my rear view mirror and wondered if my glasses were telling the truth. I was amazed that those wheels of his were still rolling. Not only was seventy-five percent of the car covered in rust, I could see he had something large hanging out of the trunk. When we arrived at the restaurant I could see the object half in and half out of the trunk was one of the largest outboard motors I had ever seen, loosely secured with an old rusted chain. So I asked, "How nice, you have a boat?"

"No," he replied, "I had a boat but I sold it. I kept the motor and don't have any room in my one-bedroom apartment to store it, so I keep it in my trunk. I got it chained up so no one can steal it during the night."

"So your trunk is always open?"

"Yea, I disconnected the light so's the battery doesn't run down."

"What if it rains," I asked, "doesn't your trunk get full of water?"

"Sure, but it drains out pretty quick because there's a hole in the bottom of it."

"You mean a drain hole Mercedes built in?"

"No, it developed on its own. You know; a rust hole."

NEXT!!

It's not easy to surprise me, but I was dumbfounded when he began to compliment my well-maintained convertible and with a proud smile on his face stated that he plans to "do me one better" by sawing off the whole top of his car so he will have an instant convertible every day of the year, and not have to "push a button" to make it happen. At that point I'm "all in" for the fun of it, thinking this guy is bonkers. We walked through the hotel lobby and onto the pool deck to the Tiki Bar. Because he's walking many steps ahead of me, he arrives first and bluntly asks the bartender for a rum and Coke. He looks at me in haste and asks, "What do you want?" I'm thinking, "Not you," but I was polite enough not to say it.

From that point on I was taking a lesson in what not to do if I am ever reborn as a man in another life:

- Don't carelessly squeeze lemon into your drink so that it actually shoots across the table into your date's eye.
- Don't order raw oysters without asking your date if she can tolerate oysters that way.
- Don't talk incessantly while eating, letting food (let alone raw oysters) dangle out while refusing to let your date get a word in edgewise.
- Don't ramble on about how you are a three-time loser at marriage and how two of your ex-wives were "mail order brides" hastily chosen late at night after a few too many rum and Cokes.
- And especially, don't mention how while working in Cuba you got gonorrhea from a local "bar-fly" and how, soon after being cured by a shot of antibiotics in the buttocks through a straw-sized needle, you went back to the same bar and got it a second time from the very same woman.

Angela LaTorre

- Don't do any of those things, unless you really, really enjoy being alone.

Forty-two minutes have now gone by since he first flagged me down from the bridge, and I thought to myself, this one takes the cake—car, outboard motor, manners, you name it.

So why wasn't I already on my way home? I'm not sure, but I am sorry. As we were leaving the restaurant—he was gracious enough to pick up the tab—he invited me to follow him to his apartment and then to the beach. He said he just came back from New York and decided to buy a "longboard" surf board. He is "dying" to try surfing once again after a thirty-five year hiatus.

If I knew why I said yes, I'd tell you. I only know that I did. His vehicle was clearly a giant mess and the condition of his little apartment was no better. It smelled of mildew because he did not run the air conditioning during July and August while he was gone. I had a vision of fungus much like what was growing under his two big toe nails. Down on the beach he tried to lure me into the ocean with him, but after making it very clear that wasn't about to happen, I watched him doing his best to replicate the surfing master he claimed to have been thirty-five years earlier on the beaches of New York and New Jersey. Surf conditions were excellent; the problem was his belly. It was the only part of his sturdy anatomy that made any contact with the board. Surprisingly, he wasn't frustrated. He was overjoyed just to be out there trying. I began to think this experience had run its course. When I told him I was heading home, he smiled and said, "How 'bout giving 'the Big Kahuna' a nice wet 'germ'," which he explained meant a big wet kiss. On that note, this girl had officially had enough; the party was over, the chapter was written and my convertible was heading back south.

NEXT!!

Without a doubt, my internet dating confidence had been challenged. The next day, Prince Charming sent a short e-mail confirming his conviction that what I needed most was to give up my body and have sex with him. He was sure that sex would have made our delightful afternoon even more memorable. Apparently, his surfing instantly improved after I departed. What a show I missed! Ironically, he ended his message by using one of my favorite words, "What's **NEXT** Angie?"

I replied, "Sorry, not you."

A few weeks went by and a gentleman I had talked to months earlier but never met contacted me and wanted to finally meet. He was a retired professional, successful, geographically desirable, and once divorced. At least that's what he said, and as usual, I took him at his word. We did have excellent phone conversations.

Our first meeting was a no-show on his part due to a medical issue that landed him in the ER. He apologized profusely and because I know unexpected things can happen, I decided to give him another chance. But having dropped the ball once, the second meeting had to be for more than milk and cookies. I named the place and he agreed we'd meet for a nice dinner. He was delighted that I was giving him a second chance.

We were to meet at 7 p.m. at the bar at *Stonewoods* in Ormond Beach, a little north of Daytona. *Stonewoods* is a favorite of mine, but I don't like sitting at any bar by myself. I took a lot of time to look as attractive as possible and he agreed to be there fifteen minutes early, "just waiting anxiously for you." We had laughed at that line and he swore he would do it. But he didn't. The roles were reversed as I waited for him again—remember, he had already stood me up once. So here I was again, waiting and no Rick. After enjoying my Mojito, an appetizer, and trying to call him with no response, I concluded I'd been stood up again by this idiot.

Coincidentally, sitting just a few bar stools away were two nice women, one of whom was an old client and a friend of the family. We recognized each other, and they asked me to join them. As the discussion unfolded, inquiring female minds forced me to admit I had been left in the dust by one "Mr. So and So." Descriptions and names followed, and as the puzzle was pieced together we concluded, much to our amazement, that "no show Rick" had been married for nineteen years to the woman accompanying my former client. He left her for a nineteen-year-old "clerk" when he turned fifty. The man cannot even walk, she said, and, "Trust me, you should consider yourself lucky that he didn't show because he's a total nightmare."

We laughed, drank and agreed it's truly a small world. **Good points**: I got my old client back, met a new friend and enjoyed some of the best Mojitos ever!

Angie's Lessons Learned ...
Once you've taken a class, it makes no sense to pay tuition to take it again.

"I was in a bar and I said to a friend, 'You know, we've become those 40-year-old guys we used to look at and say, 'Isn't it sad?'"
~ George Clooney, American actor

BAR SCENE LIES

I have never been much of a drinker, therefore "The Bar Scene" is not my cup of tea. I do not enjoy the scent of smoke or coming home smelling like a dirty ashtray. However, at this point in my life I was still new to New Smyrna Beach and trying to meet people and build my business. New Smyrna Beach is nestled between the shorelines of Ponce Inlet and The Canaveral National Park. I said in an earlier chapter that for many years it was Central Florida's best kept secret. The charm, beauty and magic it possesses are gifts to its year-round locals, winter "snow birds," and visiting inland Florida residents. It has at times been called "Orlando's Beach," although Cocoa Beach also has enjoyed that designation. It scores high for concentration of bars and restaurants as you might expect from a tourist town.

Living in a new town is conducive to meeting new girlfriends and, since not everyone is the same, to compromis-

NEXT!!

ing a bit as we all do in any relationship. One particular Saturday in April, a new friend who enjoys the bar scene and is quite a bit younger than me, wanted to check out New Smyrna Beach's finest bars and do a little bar hopping. With some apprehension, I agreed and justified it as a potential business building opportunity.

Lounge number two on our list of three was a beautifully renovated bar/restaurant. Florida law prohibits smoking in bars with food service so I welcomed a chance to just sit and talk with some nice people, two of whom were gentleman, or at least of the male persuasion. Whether they were truly gentlemen would be answered later. For simple identification purposes they will anonymously be called John and Bill. It's interesting to watch what men drink and how long it takes them to consume alcohol. As the conversations continued I noticed that John, a rather large man, was nursing a beer over the course of almost an hour. Bill on the other hand seemed to be really enjoying good old *Jack Daniels* on the rocks. At 1.5 ounces per drink, he had downed three ounces over the course of about thirty minutes, and within the first hour was starting on his third Jack on the Rocks. Consuming slow beer vs. fast Jack will make a difference in the way a man's mouth works, a woman's too I suppose, and the stories coming from fast drinking Bill began to outpace the more mellow ways of his big friend John.

Even though we continued talking together as a foursome of friends, it was clear some pairing up was starting, and I was spending more time paying attention to Bill and watching him enjoy his Jack. John, we learned, was retired, visiting the area and staying on his boat, which we later learned was really a yacht as it was over fifty feet long. John was enjoying the company of my girlfriend, and there seemed to be a nice possible connection going on. His words were clear and seemed to be truly genuine. The same couldn't be said for Bill. As he finished his third cocktail I made it clear that I was not impressed with men who seem to have a drinking problem and that alcoholism was very foreign to me. He appeared to welcome that, and declined a fourth drink. He began talking about business, which he knew was my motivation for braving "The Bar Scene." He also was from New Jersey, close to my hometown and we were close in age. Our high schools were rivals, so needless to say we did have things to talk about.

As he became more serious he explained that he had gone through a bad divorce, sold everything he had up north, and was starting his life over in beautiful New Smyrna Beach. His kids were grown and doing well and he had great business plans involving home health care. He also stated that he owned somewhat of a "mansion" on the river in nearby Edgewater, with a rental property attached that supports the mansion and pays his bills. He claimed this situation had been working well for him while he tried to get his business off the ground. It was a sudden change of style, but I was not convinced. What seemed to be really working well on him at that moment was the *Jack Daniels*, since mansions on the river in Edgewater are for the most part nonexistent. In any event, as time went on he seemed a little more sober, but remember, I am still freshly divorced at this time and very new to this whole bar scene—not to mention a touch gullible by nature. The home health care business he described was to involve personal care to elderly residents who were uninsured and needed some assistance. We spoke regarding my experience in the skin care business and how we could possibly incorporate good basic,

> I began to wonder if this guy had completely lost his grip on reality.

NEXT!!

non-medical, skin care benefits to help them take care of themselves and good preventive measures that would deter potential skin care disorders. Of course, many business ideas that seem great after three whiskeys look terrible in the light of day, and many alliances between men and woman courting each other under a sub-tropical moon turn out to be nothing more than romantic posturing. I wasn't sure where this one would lead, but he did seem to have some good ideas and assured me the business was on course and the preliminary paperwork and financial backing was in the works. We all said good night, and I realized that my friend was planning to see John again. We talked about possibly enjoying a nice trip on the yacht at some time.

    Weeks passed before I received a call from Bill one morning regarding meeting him for lunch and possibly talking a little further regarding the business. He wanted me to visit his home (the so-called mansion on the river) and talk. He obviously was proud of his properties, and of course I was curious. I put on my business suit and agreed to meet. There is one street to my knowledge in Edgewater that has water front properties, and that is Riverside Drive. His address was clearly not Riverside Drive. In my quest to find him—and thank God once again for cell phones—I finally arrived on a road that leads to Riverside Drive. When I questioned him, he assured me there was a view of the river from his place, adding with a smile that, "All Roads Lead to Water."

    He met me at the end of the driveway shared by the rental unit in the front of his property, and as I walked with him up the driveway there was something about his black high top sneakers with loose flopping tongues and red shoes laces that told me I was in for another book-worthy treat. On each side of the driveway the junk was piled high: Old tires, rusty wheelbarrows, bikes, tools, you name it—

trash and debris galore. *Sanford and Son* would have been delighted, but I was aghast. The garage behind the "mansion" was a conversion of sorts that he called his cottage. He had greeted me in a torn tee shirt, nasty shorts and of course those amazing sneakers, which now seemed to fit right in with everything else. I was dumbfounded at how some men are just so dense and have no idea what it takes to impress a woman, *and* this was to be about business as well. I mean, he had invited me and I put on a business suit! I sat down carefully in my business suit on a folding beach chair that was missing several woven straps and fit well among the other junk. Please know that I'm not a masochist; I stayed because I knew it was only going to get better and I'd once again find laughter in all this dating madness. He offered me something to drink and I said ice tea or any diet drink would be fine. He replied he had not been to the grocery story yet this week, even though we had spoken hours earlier, giving him plenty of time to prepare to play host. "I can offer you tap water with a wedge of lemon," he said. How delightful, I thought, wondering where the lemon had been. I was thirsty, especially from trying to find the "mansion," and agreed. As he headed to his kitchen I was thinking how I had pictured him living in the big house and his renter in what I'd imagined as a carriage house of sorts. Now I was wondering who was the landlord in this scenario.

 He arrived with a mason jar in his hand. The lemon looked good enough but cold was a luxury since he had no ice maker and hadn't bothered yet to buy any ice cube trays. I wondered what would be his next little amusement. The beach chair was holding up OK, but now he announced it was time for the grand tour of his cottage/garage apartment. I was still waiting for the river view. As the minutes passed, I began to wonder if this guy had completely lost his grip on

NEXT!!

reality. Was he enjoying things stronger than good old *Jack Daniels*? He seemed to believe I wouldn't notice how we'd stepped down from a "mansion on the river" to a semi-converted garage. He had to be smoking something!

The tour began with great fanfare. I was thinking that maybe back in New Jersey he had worked as a carnival barker on the midway, the kind of guy who could convince you a poor woman with psoriasis was really half alligator. The tour continued. The two-car garage was littered with old area rugs and wasn't even divided into rooms. His "conversion to a cottage" involved hanging vinyl shower curtains to strategically separate the garage into three smaller areas. I think I saw an episode of *The Three Stooges* where they all got married and did something quite similar with their living quarters. I will admit he managed to have running water and did a good job placing a functioning bathroom in the garage, but I was still waiting for that view of the river. After complimenting him on his collection of "Early Garage Sale" furniture, I was ready for "The View." I couldn't stop thinking about the difference between him and John, with whom my friend could possibly be enjoying a real view of the water right now. I was wondering, just wishing and wondering.

But my curiosity about Bill's "river view" was about to be cured. Upon inquiring in a rather diplomatic way, he proceeded to escort me to "the rental unit" in the front of the property (remember he was supposedly the landlord but living in the garage). The three bedroom, two bath stucco main house dated from the early 70's and was really just an average Florida home. Not a mansion in any way. It was in ill repair, but he promised me it was perfectly placed to afford a view of the river. The water view did indeed exist. I actually believed him, but how and from where? Passing through the cluttered interior, in the absence of the tenant, we entered one of the two baths. We stopped and he folded his arms across his chest, stating with a pompous air of triumph, "Now Angie, if you will step to the right side of the toilet and look to your right through the small window you will see the color blue. That, my lady, is the river." I cannot tell you how difficult it was for me not to explode in a world of laughter as I thought to myself, "another great chapter, but people will think I made it up!" But sure enough, good old *Jack Daniels* drinking Bill was right, there was a spot of blue out there the size of a index card.

I thanked him for his time and asked how things were going regarding the business. I really didn't want to hear what I knew would be another bogus story but I had to ask, although what I truly wanted was a fast exit. He babbled something about waiting for the initial process to begin as licensing was underway and ... *yada, yada,* he would be in touch. I told him, "No," I would be in touch instead. "In touch" meaning I wouldn't touch him with a ten-foot pole as a business partner, date or even a friend. This is all true, I promise you. I said goodbye and carefully backed out of the dirt driveway, avoiding any encounters with his rusty junk.

The moral to this chapter is to take note of how men in bars handle their liquor. Are *they* in control, or the alcohol? When the liquor flows, the lies are sure to flow with it. My best advice is to avoid the bar scene altogether. **NEXT!!**

Good points: He confirmed what an old minister once told me, "What you find in a bar you will lose in a Bar."

Angie's Lessons Learned ...
Drinking to excess is often self-deception. So why not deceive others as well?

*"I'm the kind of man who deserves to have women
I don't deserve."*
~ Anonymous pick-up line

EASY PICK-UPS AND THE PLAYER

I've always found it interesting to hear the creative ways men try to pick up women. In most cases a woman can only be "picked up" if that is what she wants. Most men can tell right away. I have been fortunate to have many single male friends, clients (who I never date), dancing friends and handyman friends who helped maintain my rental units. So on occasion, just for background knowledge, I would chat with them to discover the secrets of male thinking, right or wrong, on picking up women.

Here's what they told me: If a woman sits at a bar alone, it's obvious she is available and would welcome the idea of being pursued. If a woman in a social setting is dressed in a provocative manner, and if she is scanning the room and focusing in on individual men, she is obviously looking for attention. One of my good friends who has been single and dating for a long time said to me, "Angie if a man is inter-

NEXT!!

ested in a long-term meaningful relationship, he doesn't mind doing the chasing—which involves time and expense—as long as the woman wants to be caught. I have never forgotten that. A woman should not pretend to want to be caught just for the fun of being pursued. It's not a crime, but I do believe total honesty is so important in life and relationships. I'd put communication at number two, and respect at number three, which includes men being total gentlemen. Number three becomes especially important if in time the relationship becomes a physical one. Mutual consideration is always key in a relationship of caring equals.

Anyway, back to the art of the pick-up, the lines men use, and their crazy methods: The winter of 2008 was well upon me and I was in Daytona Beach pumping gas (in my car, not as a job!). I had doctor appointments scheduled along with a business luncheon that day so I was dressed nicely. I was wearing my red wool wrap-around dress—a classic I have had for fifteen years. It fits close to the body but is very tasteful, showing just a hint of cleavage. The dress happened to match the vintage red *Mercedes Benz* I drive and apparently caught the attention of a rather prominent businessman from Orlando. He was in Volusia County for the day, "bird watching" he claimed. Well, the last time I checked I didn't have wings. Anyway, he approached and began to compliment me on the dress, the matching car and on and on. He offered to clean my windshield and check my oil. No thanks, I replied and then, as often happens, a business conversation ensued. He appeared to be interested in my services and of course being self-employed and learning to survive on my own, I am always promoting my services. I gave

> He obviously did not have a clue who he was talking to. I was no longer as naïve as I once was.

him a business card, thanked him for the compliments and said goodbye.

A few weeks passed. I had been pursuing possible job opportunities in the Lake Mary/Longwood area, closer to Orlando, because my practice just wasn't developing as I wished in New Smyrna Beach—despite its older demographics that one might think would be interested in skin care but generally isn't. Anyway, "Mr. Player" called and said he'd like to meet me for lunch as he would be in my area once again, "bird watching." I happened to have appointments again that day, but agreed to meet him because he claimed to have many contacts from Lake Mary to Winter Park. He described himself as a longtime resident of Winter Park, an upscale Orlando suburb, and the owner three very popular bar/restaurant locations. He was well spoken on the phone, nice looking and had the confidence of someone whose accomplishments are real. Of course, there was more to the story. In hindsight I have learned it's very easy for a man to be a "player" when he has money and can conveniently leave his home territory to play.

As a general rule, be very careful with men on the internet who post no photos and give insufficient information for their wives to connect the dots. "Mr. Player" tells me to select the finest restaurant in Daytona Beach, make a reservation, and promises to arrive in a timely manner. I decided (as usual) to say, "Why not!" What trouble could I get in? A restaurant is a public place and I had wanted to try this beautiful new place directly facing the ocean in a lovely resort hotel. Reservations made, I arrived and was shown to our table, where I chose a fine, high-end white wine. I was about to enjoy a delectable lobster appetizer when "The Player" called to announce he would be a few minutes late, adding that I should order a nice bottle of wine and start

NEXT!!

without him. I was two steps ahead of him.

 He arrived sporting no evidence of bird watching attire, wearing expensive cologne, nicely shaved with a fresh haircut. A forgotten trace of a significant accessory, however, was the tan line from his dismissed wedding band. I noticed it right away and inquired. He freely admitted being married and shamelessly stated that "it should have been obvious to me," and that of course he "had every intention of telling me." So brazen, it was amazing. I will say the lobster was good and the wine better. Small talk about business followed and then it was time for my version of "Q and A." So why are you here? How is the wife? A good woman, I'm sure. And tell me about the children? And lastly do you always try to pick up women in red dresses pumping gas?

 As a veteran "bird watcher" he was very well versed at the art; a highly skilled player, he was ready to respond with whatever he thought would be acceptable answers. He obviously did not have a clue who he was talking to. I was no longer as naïve as I once was, and it was clear that his bird watching was the kind practiced by barnyard roosters.

 With the truth now out, he was only too glad to tell his glorious story. He was so successful, with such good employees, that all he had to do was be the chief bean counter for his three businesses, collect the spoils and enjoy having his free time away from home with all the toys some men love—like boats, motorcycles, and women on the side, it seemed. His wife, he said with a pride that belied his betrayal of her, "Is a former model, beautiful, and a great mother to our ten-year-old." An honor roll student at a private school, he boasted. His beautiful home in Winter Park is maintained by staff and life is so grand. Almost as grand as he is full of himself, I thought. So why all this, I asked, the cheating and lying to both his wife and me? His response: "I like to stir the pot, and baby I like what I am looking at."

I was once again aghast and said, "Really, that makes it OK?" I told him a bit about myself and how I felt cheating is the lowest and worst thing you could do to your mate. He disagreed and said, "It's just fun." I thanked him for lunch and advised him to go home and stir that home pot, thinking—and maybe even hoping—that a bad burn was on his horizon. I truly feel in the end the result of infidelity is never a good one; the hurt is tremendous and the kids always get the worst of it. Beyond all measure, he was a **NEXT!!** I asked him to never call me again and I would not be able to ever step foot in his restaurants again, knowing what he is all about.

Good points: None. This man was a complete sociopath. Somewhere in the Bible Jesus says God lets bad fortune fall equally on both the good and the evil, and I guess it's the same for good fortune. But when I see someone so selfish doing so well, I just wish it wasn't so.

Angie's Lessons Learned ...
Sometimes it's wise to just assume a man is married until he proves he's not.

"If a rich man is proud of his wealth, he should not be praised until it is known how he employs it."
~ Socrates, Ancient Greek Philosopher

MR. MONEY BUCKS

As time progressed I tried hard to digest everything I had learned from dating so many men who clearly were not what I was looking for. Was I setting my sights too low and dating men I should never have agreed to date? Or was I asking too much of the men I dated and thereby sabotaging any chance for a good relationship? I didn't have an answer I could count on, but I hadn't given up. I was continuing to enjoy time with girlfriends and friends in the dance community. And I remained open to meeting "Mr. Right" at any time.

As these things go, I found myself entertaining the thought of meeting a gentleman that a trusted girlfriend of mine knew on a friendly basis. At this point in my dating experience I thought maybe meeting a man with money would be a good idea. It's been said that it's just as easy to fall in love with a rich man as a poor man, and my liaisons

NEXT!!

with "pretty boys" like "The Surfer" and "The Scam Artist" hadn't paid off that well. I had never specifically decided to date someone just because they had money, but many women I know would speak of money as such an important factor in what they are seeking in a man. I was curious, so I agreed to meet "Mr. Money Bucks."

Typically, men with money tend to be a bit "seasoned" as well. "Mr. Money Bucks" had just turned sixty-five and had the privilege of full retirement after an acclaimed career as a captain with a major commercial airline prior to "9/11."

Trusting my friend, I agreed to our first date after a long and encouraging phone call with my latest prospect. He was indeed "seasoned," but rather nice looking and of course, as I would come to expect later, he wanted to meet at a bar well stocked with his favorite elixir, *Crown Royal*. His second statement after an initial hello was, "Don't worry, order what you want, I have money." I was duly impressed and we seemed to enjoy a rather lively evening. He enjoyed his *Crown Royal*, which the bartender kept flowing, but remained very controlled. I left in my own car with a second date with him already planned. Again trusting my friend and based on our pleasant first date and factors like his apparent love for his daughters and two ex-wives, I agreed to join him for dinner at his home.

He was rightfully proud of his beautiful home on the river. The seven thousand square feet were incredibly adorned with art gathered during his travels. A one thousand square foot bar/party room dominated the very top floor. It was quite the bachelor pad. The *Crown Royal* was being enjoyed a little more than what I usually appreciate, but I thought, he's at home so I guess it's acceptable. But although we were sharing laughs in the lap of luxury I felt troubled by my surroundings. His home felt more like a house than a home.

Angela LaTorre

There was a true sense of loneliness there. I have never understood the need for so much space for one person. In any event, it was truly grand and so was dinner. He shared his life story and the tour of the home included many memories. Along the way he recounted his extravagant retirement party that was held in Atlanta with a price tag of $20,000, which he paid entirely from his own pocket. I always wonder when someone tells of spending great sums of money as if it was nothing at all; if it's really nothing at all why are they mentioning the amount? Obviously, this man's accomplishments and his money, maybe mostly his money, were basically what he saw as his true being.

The third date for me seems always to be the one that determines if a fourth date is in the cards. Well, our third date was indeed the last date. I decided I would ask him to a big family birthday party for my sister because once again I was tired of going to functions alone. I have since learned to wait a considerable amount of time before doing the family introduction thing. As a matter of fact, he was the last man to be introduced to my family for several years. They still talk about that night, so here goes: He arrives with a bottle of *Crown Royal* in hand, but not presented as a gift for other guests to enjoy. Along with the large size bottle, two glasses appeared that were engraved as follows: "Captain" and "Co-Captain." You can figure out the rest. My family watched this unfold, and they tease me about the retired pilot to this day. I have since concluded that, to one degree or another, most pilots are binge drinkers. This seems to come naturally, considering they are not allowed to drink for eight hours before a flight and are deprived while in the

> Sometimes a girl might want to lie down, but at other times she just wants to lay down the law.

NEXT!!

air. And, of course, once they land, plenty of bar stools are waiting nearby.

Despite his arrogance, the party was fun; but on our way home he openly stated that by now I should fully understand that in this book, as far as we are concerned, I need to be aware that there are guidelines, rules, and "the law," and those three things are not the same. Guidelines and rules are OK for a girl like me, he says, but he represents "the law," and on the third date his law book demands sex. Well "Mr. Money Bucks," we obviously have two different law books. Sometimes a girl might want to lie down, but at other times she just wants to lay down the law. This was the latter case, since I was already annoyed by his heavy drinking ways and by his taking the remaining *Crown Royal* home with him, which in my eyes is totally cheap and classless. His confident description of "the law" petered out as we pulled into his three-car garage and I exited with my car keys in hand. I let him know what I thought of him as I said farewell and stated that I was far from ready to have a physical relationship with him.

There was no mistaking the pleasure I felt when I told him maybe he could consummate his "laws" with someone he really loves, for example ... himself! No more drinking pilots for me, however rich they might be.

The lesson learned for me was money does not automatically create happiness and can be a real issue when there's an extreme financial difference between two people. Men like "Mr. Money Bucks" believe in their own "Golden Rule," that is "he who has the gold makes the rules." He tried to use his money and career accomplishments to control, but it doesn't work with this girl. I suspect he'll spend the rest of his life alone, "buying" his little self-gratifying trysts until he can't handle it anymore. **NEXT!!** ... in a big way!

Angela LaTorre

Good points: He filled a few gaps in my education as he described the art work in his home. That's all folks. In my mind, the jury is still out on whether it's just as easy to love a rich man—especially if love is what you really want and not money.

> **Angie's Lessons Learned ...**
> Wanting to find a guy who's financially stable makes sense. Chasing money doesn't.

> *"Let us be grateful to people who make us happy; they are the charming gardeners who make our souls blossom."*
> ~ Marcel Proust, French Author

THE ENGLISH DELIGHT

I am going to admit something you probably have already noticed: Throughout all my dating adventures, I was never just "dating." I was always in search of "Mr. Right." Maybe that was the wrong approach. In fact, friends said to me, "Why not just date people casually and try to enjoy yourself. Who needs marriage?" Well, the answer to that question is, "me!" When I see that a man isn't a good candidate for matrimony, whether that takes one night or four months, it's time to say, **NEXT!!** The one exception might have been the gentleman I call the "English Delight." I think I knew it wasn't going anywhere the very first evening we met, but I just plain enjoyed his company.

I met "the English Delight" while visiting my family in South Florida. The dance floor was calling to me and whenever I'm in South Florida the *Gold Coast Ballroom* is always on my "to do" list. *Gold Coast* mixes a remarkable ambience

NEXT!!

with a collection of international people, many of whom are among the best dancers in Florida on a "pro/am" level. Feeling a bit curious, I was lured into the arms of a rather striking gentleman who turned out to be a native Englishman. His ways were very European and his Rod Stewart accent was highly addicting. The connection and attraction between us was magical and instant—despite his age. He was a professional musician who had traveled the world working on cruise ships and had a voice that reminded me of the Canadian singer Michael Bublé.

> It was part of our romantic fantasy that someday I'd visit him in England.

My English gentleman—he was indeed quite the suave gentleman—lived in Boca Raton and was planning to go back to England soon to be with his aging mother. He was charming and a pleasure to be with so I continued our occasional dating right up to his departure for England. We agreed that someday I would visit him in England, and it was part of our romantic fantasy that we both believed it would happen. I decided to add this short chapter as a bit of a reminder to focus on what's really important as far as the qualities one desires in a life partner, and not to be easily lured by looks, charm and an oh-so-sexy English accent. You might have fun for a while but while you're playing, the real love of your life might pass right by.

Angie's Lessons Learned ...
If you keep traveling down side streets, you'll never reach your destination.

> *"Never taunt the alligator until after you've crossed the river."*
> ~ Belizean Proverb

THE GATOR

I gave him the name "Gator" because he was a big fan of the highly acclaimed University of Florida football Gators, and for a while I thought maybe he'd be my National Champion. "The Gator" had promise and took the prize of lasting the longest—six months—before the final bell rang and he too went out the door labeled NEXT! I wish him well because he did indeed have many redeeming qualities.

Gator was a handsome man of great German stature, standing six-foot-five and wearing a size 52-long sport coat. When the Gator entered a room, everyone noticed. With his warm smile the first impression was always good, but by the time he left the opinion had often changed. The Gator held extreme right wing political views and he liked to express them with a confidence that he was always correct. Add in his size and he could be unbearable. Coaxing the good out

NEXT!!

of him while discouraging the bad was almost a full-time job. But all in all our six months together were well worth it. He was full of surprises and romance, and his heart—at least for me—was in the right place. His two beautiful daughters were the love of his life and I admired that. He was a big teddy bear with a tender heart. He always arrived with a gift in hand and was very attentive.

Maybe by this time my expectations had dwindled, but despite his shortcomings I truly believed things were progressing nicely. Then he invited me to visit "The Swamp" in Gainesville to attend the spring football "blue and orange" game. As an alumni with a daughter currently enrolled at "UF," he was in "Gator Heaven" as he prepared to attend the spring game. But this was also the first time that I was completely in his world. Up to this point we had played by my rules. Well, we hooked up with some of his old Gator friends, and as the game progressed and the *Wild Turkey* bourbon began to flow, unbridled passion began to take over. It was a hot day and he claimed he was just thirsty, but to my eyes he seemed out of his mind crazy. I began to have doubts. Sure, it was great to see a man having a really great time, but on the other hand the day was revealing some of his faults. For one thing, I naturally recoil from excessive drinking, mostly because it makes me fear for my safety. In addition, you have to wonder when a man invites you for a day-long outing two and a half hours away and then depends on you to make it happen. We had to take my car because his is very old with bad tires and other mechanical problems. He didn't want to see us broken down alongside the road, he explained, as if he was only thinking of me. And then, when we arrived at the stadium, he was startled to learn it would cost $10 for the two of us to get in. Seems he left home with no cash.

But we got past it. Sure, he was fumbling the ball now and then but he always managed to recover. Soon after our day at "The Swamp," he took me to Orlando to see the musical *Jersey Boys*, which I have to say was the highlight of our six months together. They were expensive tickets and I knew he must have scrimped on his own pleasures to afford them. His mom was very ill at that time and living in a nursing home where he visited often. With his other responsibilities he had a lot on his plate, but he was very careful to include me in his life.

Weeks had passed before I finally decided to see how and where he lived. They say if you really want to know someone visit them in their home. So I set out to see my teddy bear in his own lair. I was concerned when I first heard he was living "temporarily" in his mom's home, and that he would not let me enter his own house. After a quick drive by I could see why. The neighborhood was generally run down, and his house fit right in. "Eventually, I'll get it fixed up," he assured me, adding that he really "wanted" to do the work himself. Well, he was rebuilding his life after his divorce and having two girls in college is very taxing on the old balance sheet, so I said I understood and we continued.

> ... This was not a good thing to say to any woman of Italian descent ...

The deal-breaker, however, came in the early spring as I was keeping my two young grandsons. I had committed to watching the boys while my son and daughter enjoyed a vacation in Greece. The Gator was invited to a family graduation party, his second family gathering, and of course the two boys were with us. The evening was full of proud moments as my nephew, who had overcome serious medical issues to finish in the top ten in his class, celebrated his graduation from Florida State University—chief rival of "UF"

NEXT!!

and the Gator. Claims and counter-claims were flying—all in good fun—as the storied rivalry played out at the party. As we were getting ready to leave, my four-year-old grandson became emotional when his shoes ended up missing and all hell broke loose between the Gator and me. You might say he showed his "blue and orange" blood in a very unattractive way and I was not about to take it. Obviously not impressed with my "Nona skills," he lectured me as we walked out the door, "It's a good thing we didn't meet when our children were young because we have different views on how to raise children. We'd have never made it." This was not a good thing to say to me—or to any girl of Italian descent, because our families are everything to us. Sticking his nose in where my grandchildren were involved was a perfect way for him to get his Gator snout bitten off.

When unhappiness sets into my heart, my tears flow and relief has to be found. I believe soup needs to stew but not people. So I called him and let him know he was out of line. He apologized and said he was determined to make it right, which I believed because I knew he really cared for me and was hoping for a future together.

The following Sunday was Mother's Day. After eleven days with a two- and four-year-old, and having been up most of the night, I was exhausted but still delighted to have had so much quality time with those two incredible boys. (Doesn't every grandmother think her grandsons are incredible?) But I was too tired to load the car to visit my own mother, so I called and apologized, which she understood. At that moment the Gator called with a peace offering: "I'll be over around 4 p.m. with popcorn, movies, games and, of course, me. You can get caught up on your rest." That sounded good because the next day I planned to travel south to meet my daughter and turn the grandsons over to her.

Angela LaTorre

The Gator arrived in his usual glory and was a welcome sight. His long, large arms held goodies galore. When I take the boys into my home, watching the family dog is always part of the deal. I usually keep him sequestered where he can't make a mess, but trying to soften his image as strict disciplinarian, the Gator suggested we let the dog join in the family fun. The pet lover in him was calling as well as he argued for letting their little dog in. I have good reason to keep little "Spicy" confined. For one thing, he's a highly valuable animal who loves nothing more than to spot an open door and bolt for the great outdoors. Beyond that, he's terribly hyper, untrained and—I hate to say it— just plain crazy. Definitely more of a challenge that the boys.

The TV I keep upstairs in my bedroom is the only one with a DVD player, and as the Gator was slowly coming down the stairs with the TV in hand so they could watch *Aladdin* downstairs, the boys were in a state of high excitement over all the goodies brought by their new friend, the Gator. Spicy was off the wall and decided to do his business on step number five as the Gator was on step number four. Since Spicy is about the size of my massive friend's shoe, he was unaware any of this was happening. The boys start screaming, "Nona, Spicy kaka!" ... which you may know is a kind of Spanish/Italian slang for poop. Of course, Anglo Gator was clueless and in his mind, my grandsons were speaking gibberish. Too late! The Gator steps right in the unexpected surprise, slips and almost goes down. Precarious, to say the least! I still don't know how he managed to right himself and not drop the television set, but he did. Still, he was not at all happy.

Hours later, all was at peace. Spicy was back in solitary confinement where he belongs, bellies were full, *Aladdin* had helped suppress the negative energy, and "Nona" had taken her much needed nap. But on that day and over the days that followed, I felt confirmed in my decision that the Gator was not a good fit for me and my family. Six months, at least in this book, is a long time and I'd have to say compared to most of my relationships, this could honestly be called a love affair. In the beginning, when our passions flowed, he made me feel like a new bride. But in the end he began to treat me like a dominated wife: Not a good plan for winning my lasting affection. **NEXT!!**

Good points: Now when I hear people talking about "The Swamp" at the University of Florida, I can say I was there and experienced the meaning of "bleeding blue and orange." I wish him all the best.

Angie's Lessons Learned ...
Watch out for cultural differences, whether they have to do with football or family.

> *"I am extraordinarily patient, provided I get my own way in the end."*
> ~ Margaret Thatcher, British Prime Minister

THE HOPEFUL FINALE

I didn't begin writing this book until after I'd already put quite a few men on the list titled NEXT!! But I always hoped I would be able to finish with optimism and report that I'd finally found the right guy for me. Well, I recently met a wonderful man while visiting a local dance place called the *Rockin' Ranch*. He is a nice looking man, although not as tall as I thought I wanted and with less hair than I always imagined for my Prince. He did meet my basic requirements by being just a bit taller than me and certainly weighing more than I do. I guess he made me realize how foolish my surface criteria really were. When I looked deep into his eyes, his compassionate warmth came shining through. Being close to him made the butterflies within me dance again. As I touched his hand he smiled at me and said, "So tell me what kind of woman are you." No, we haven't yet made altar plans but he immediately captured my interest and the feelings have grown stronger and stronger ever since.

NEXT!!

Over the past four and a half years I had met several men in a bar setting but their approach was usually like what I reported in "Bar Room Lies." They were always trying to puff themselves up. This one was the first to ask me who I am. He appeared to be looking for the right woman, not just any woman for a quick thrill. At this point, he is everything I have been looking for and more. For the first time in my life since my Dad passed in 1996, I feel like a Princess and I feel in my heart it will continue. Time will tell. Surprises pop up in relationships. Sometimes they can be overcome; other times they can't.

I conclude with a message to all of you who decide in your head what's most important: Listen more to your heart. A beautiful gift may come wrapped in a plain paper package, but what's inside is a true treasure. Don't seek perfection; you probably won't even know what is perfect for you until it comes your way. Ideal perfection doesn't exist outside of heaven. Follow your heart and listen for spiritual guidance.

Angie's Lessons Learned ...
The more you fret over what you want, the less you know about what you need.

"The most important thing in life is to learn how to give out love, and to let it come in."
~ Morrie Schwartz, American educator

WHERE ARE YOU?

Where are you? Don't you think that every woman who is out there looking for "Mr. Right" has asked that question, maybe even screamed it in desperation? As I mentioned in the last chapter, I'm hoping I've found my answer. We'll see. What I do know is that the answer I found is not the answer I expected.

Experience really is the great teacher and we do learn from our mistakes. I went for pretty boys like "the Surfer" and "the Scam Artist." I looked up to big men like "Tall, Dark and Then Some" and "the Gator." I got caught up by adventurers like "the Biker" and was charmed by stylish older men like "the Seasoned Gentleman" and "the English Delight." I hooked up with smooth dancers, slick talkers and outright liars. I treated some relationships as serious for far too long when I should have seen much earlier they wouldn't work in the long run. I even got drawn in by men with money and dated some guys I wouldn't have dated if I wasn't so lonely and afraid. Yes, you all know what I mean, afraid of

NEXT!!

being alone forever. And all the time all I truly wanted was an honest, stable man with a heart.

I met men while ballroom dancing, in bars, online and by pure chance. I was "fixed up" by well meaning friends and family who didn't seemed to have a clue what kind of man was right for me. Sometimes I didn't either. Through it all I held on to my personal belief that after divorce it's not natural to spend the rest of one's life alone without a partner. I know for sure it's not God's plan for me.

> It's my personal belief that after divorce it's not natural to spend the rest of one's life alone without a partner. I know for sure it's not God's plan for me.

I have learned a lot about men, and more about myself. Its been an amazing journey. The path I've traveled has confirmed there is no perfect male, just as there is no perfect female. Is it any surprise that when we set out to find romance we tend to romanticize?

Rather than ask, "Where are you," maybe I should ask, "What is it I really want from life?" It's a simple question, but so many times simple proves to be best. The answer could be just as uncomplicated: I want to be loved, cared about, and cared for. I want a life that's full of joy, and someone with whom I can share it and be partners in making it real. If you are a woman who is "out there" looking, I believe you'll agree. I hope your search goes faster than mine.

Angela LaTorre Nickell

Best Wishes & Happy Dating!!
Angie

ISBN 978-0-9822819-2-5